C#.NET SOURCE CODE: WBEMSCRIPTING EXECNOTIFICATIONQUERY ASYNC

___InstanceOperationEvent

Richard Edwards

CONTENTS

INTRODUCTION

This book is constructed in a rather unique way.

Most books are, by nature, are written by subject experts who are very good at what they do. Very few are written by real programmers.

Programmers are the druids of computer programming. They tend to be soft spoken and easy going. Very focused and not wandering far from the computer keyboard.

I am neither one.

I am a writer who has been a programmer, developer and a solution expert for over the past 30 years. And as such, I am wanting to share my work with you in a rather unique way.

The book was written around the work contained in one module that from top to bottom comes out to 1850 lines of tested and reusable code. It was written in roughly 2 hours and it will take me the better part of a day for me to explain what each routine does and how you can make the routine more robust.

I can't do all of the work for you. Your own personal touch can go a long- ways.

There are also 10 pages of code which will help you create a physical overview of all namespaces and classes that is currently on your dev box. Beyond that, the rest of the work in this book is designed to be called by a form with the intent to produce reusable code.

Unfortunately, many of the routines in this book are also dedicated in that they must be used by the Win32_Process. But you can and should be able to see where changing the word Process to Bios, ComputerSystem, Product, or over 700 other names can easily turn the routines into something else entirely different.

WHAT WMI NAMESPACES AND CLASSES ARE ON YOUR MACHINE?

Someone once said, "It is what you don't know that can kill you," Well, they might not have said it exactly that way, but you get the idea.

How can you use something that exists on your machine, but you don't know it?

Back in 2002, I created something called the WMI Explorer. Microsoft came out with their version in May of 2003. Neither one of us cared, It pretty much fell flat on its face.

The biggest difference between the two is my class groupings was based on the way the classes were presented. In-other-words, I there was no underscore, the category was the classname. If there was an underscore at the beginning of the classname, it was a superclass. It there was an underscore in the middle of the classname, the letters before the underscore became its category.

I thought it was a pretty good idea at the time.

Apparently, no one else did. Fact is, the concept was never used by anyone else and WMI Explorer that other people began to "create" used the Microsoft template and never did consider a more granular approach.

I also think the other reason why the WMI Explorer didn't become popular was because of the lack of documentation beyond the most common root: root\cimv2. And back in 2003 time, there were less than a few hundred of them.

But today is a completely different ballpark. Today there are literally hundreds of classes under root\cimv2 alone.

Would you like your own personal copy?

The following scripts that I've been using since 2002, will make that happen for you. Just create a folder on your desktop, then copy and paste the three scripts into that directory and start with namespaces.vbs and end with classes.vbs.

NAMESPACES.VBS

```
Dim fso
Dim l
Dim s


EnumNamespaces("root")

Sub EnumNamespaces(ByVal nspace)

Set ws = CreateObject("Wscript.Shell")
Set fso = CreateObject("Scripting.FilesystemObject")

If fso.folderExists(ws.currentDirectory & "\" & nspace) = false then
fso.CreateFolder(ws.currentDirectory & "\" & nspace)
End If

On error Resume Next

Set      objs      =      GetObject("Winmgmts:\\.\" &
nspace).InstancesOf("__Namespace", &H20000)

If err.Number <> 0 Then
err.Clear
Exit Sub
End If

For each obj in objs
```

```vbscript
        EnumNamespaces(nspace & "\" & obj.Name)
        Next

        End Sub
```

Categories.VBS

```vbscript
        Dim fso
        Dim l
        Dim s

        Set ws = CreateObject("Wscript.Shell")
        Set fso = CreateObject("Scripting.FilesystemObject")

        EnumNamespaces("root")


        Sub EnumNamespaces(ByVal nspace)

        EnumCategories(nspace)

        If fso.folderExists(ws.currentDirectory & "\" & nspace) = false then
        fso.CreateFolder(ws.currentDirectory & "\" & nspace)
        End If

        On error Resume Next

        Set         objs        =            GetObject("Winmgmts:\\.\"        &
        nspace).InstancesOf("__Namespace", &H20000)

        If err.Number <> 0 Then
        err.Clear
        Exit Sub
```

```
End If

For each obj in objs

EnumNamespaces(nspace & "\" & obj.Name)

Next

End Sub

Sub EnumCategories(ByVal nspace)

Set ws = CreateObject("Wscript.Shell")
Set fso = CreateObject("Scripting.FilesystemObject")

Set objs = GetObject("Winmgmts:\\.\" & nspace).SubClassesOf("", &H20000)
For each obj in objs

pos = instr(obj.Path_.class, "_")

if pos = 0 then
If fso.folderExists(ws.currentDirectory & "\" & nspace & "\" & obj.Path_.Class)
= false then
fso.CreateFolder(ws.currentDirectory & "\" & nspace & "\" & obj.Path_.Class)
End If
else
if pos = 1 then
If fso.folderExists(ws.currentDirectory & "\" & nspace & "\SuperClasses") =
false then
fso.CreateFolder(ws.currentDirectory & "\" & nspace & "\SuperClasses")
End If
else
```

```vbscript
    If    fso.folderExists(ws.currentDirectory    &    "\"    &    nspace    &    "\"    &
Mid(obj.Path_.Class, 1, pos-1)) = false then
        fso.CreateFolder(ws.currentDirectory    &    "\"    &    nspace    &    "\"    &
Mid(obj.Path_.Class, 1, pos-1))
    End If
    End If
    End If


    Next


    End Sub
```

Classes.VBS

```vbscript
    Dim fso
    Dim l
    Dim s

    EnumNamespaces("root")

    Sub EnumNamespaces(ByVal nspace)

    EnumClasses(nspace)

    Set ws = CreateObject("Wscript.Shell")
    Set fso = CreateObject("Scripting.FilesystemObject")

    If fso.folderExists(ws.currentDirectory & "\" & nspace) = false then
    fso.CreateFolder(ws.currentDirectory & "\" & nspace)
    End If

    On error Resume Next
```

```
        Set         objs         =              GetObject("Winmgmts:\\.\"         &
nspace).InstancesOf("___Namespace", &H20000)

    If err.Number <> 0 Then
    err.Clear
    Exit Sub
    End If

    For each obj in objs

    EnumNamespaces(nspace & "\" & obj.Name)

    Next

    End Sub

    Sub EnumClasses(ByVal nspace)

    Set ws = CreateObject("Wscript.Shell")
    Set fso = CreateObject("Scripting.FilesystemObject")

    Set objs = GetObject("Winmgmts:\\.\" & nspace).SubClassesOf("", &H20000)
    For each obj in objs

    pos = instr(obj.Path_.class, "_")

    if pos = 0 then
        call   CreateXMLFile(ws.CurrentDirectory  &  "\"  &  nspace  &  "\"  &
obj.Path_.Class, nspace, obj.Path_.Class)
    else
    if pos = 1 then
```

```
       call CreateXMlFile(ws.CurrentDirectory & "\" & nspace & "\Superclasses",
nspace, obj.Path_.Class)
       else
       call    CreateXMLFile(ws.CurrentDirectory   &   "\"   &   nspace   &   "\"   &
Mid(obj.Path_.Class, 1, pos-1), nspace, obj.Path_.Class)
       End If
       End If

       Next

       End Sub

       Sub CreateXMLFile(ByVal Path, ByVal nspace, ByVal ClassName)


       Set fso = CreateObject("Scripting.FileSystemObject")
       Dim shorty
       On error Resume Next
       shorty = fso.GetFolder(Path).ShortPath
       If err.Number <> 0 then
       err.Clear
       Exit Sub
       End IF


       set obj = GetObject("Winmgmts:\\.\" & nspace).Get(classname)

       Set txtstream = fso.OpenTextFile(Shorty & "\" & Classname & ".xml", 2, true, -
2)
       txtstream.WriteLine("<data>")
       txtstream.WriteLine(" <NamespaceInformation>")
       txtstream.WriteLine("  <namespace>" & nspace & "</namespace>")
```

```
txtstream.WriteLine("    <classname>" & classname & "</classname>")
txtstream.WriteLine("  </NamespaceInformation>")
txtstream.WriteLine("  <properties>")

for each prop in obj.Properties_
txtstream.WriteLine("        <property Name = """" & prop.Name & """"
IsArray="""" & prop.IsArray & """" DataType = """" &
prop.Qualifiers_("CIMType").Value & """"/>")
Next
txtstream.WriteLine("  </properties>")
txtstream.WriteLine("</data>")
txtstream.close

End sub
```

As shown below, once these routines are done, you should be able to go to the folder, based on what I've told you about the Namespace\category\classes

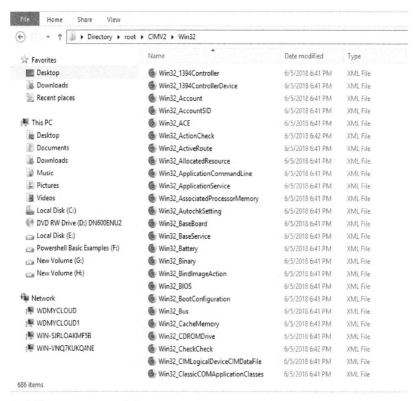

And If you open one of these up:

- <data>
  - <NamespaceInformation>
      <namespace>root\CIMV2</namespace>
      <classname>Win32_BIOS</classname>
    </NamespaceInformation>
  - <properties>
      <property Name="BiosCharacteristics" IsArray="True" DataType="uint16"/>
      <property Name="BIOSVersion" IsArray="True" DataType="string"/>
      <property Name="BuildNumber" IsArray="False" DataType="string"/>
      <property Name="Caption" IsArray="False" DataType="string"/>
      <property Name="CodeSet" IsArray="False" DataType="string"/>
      <property Name="CurrentLanguage" IsArray="False" DataType="string"/>
      <property Name="Description" IsArray="False" DataType="string"/>
      <property Name="IdentificationCode" IsArray="False" DataType="string"/>
      <property Name="InstallableLanguages" IsArray="False" DataType="uint16"/>
      <property Name="InstallDate" IsArray="False" DataType="datetime"/>
      <property Name="LanguageEdition" IsArray="False" DataType="string"/>
      <property Name="ListOfLanguages" IsArray="True" DataType="string"/>
      <property Name="Manufacturer" IsArray="False" DataType="string"/>
      <property Name="Name" IsArray="False" DataType="string"/>
      <property Name="OtherTargetOS" IsArray="False" DataType="string"/>
      <property Name="PrimaryBIOS" IsArray="False" DataType="boolean"/>
      <property Name="ReleaseDate" IsArray="False" DataType="datetime"/>
      <property Name="SerialNumber" IsArray="False" DataType="string"/>
      <property Name="SMBIOSBIOSVersion" IsArray="False" DataType="string"/>
      <property Name="SMBIOSMajorVersion" IsArray="False" DataType="uint16"/>
      <property Name="SMBIOSMinorVersion" IsArray="False" DataType="uint16"/>
      <property Name="SMBIOSPresent" IsArray="False" DataType="boolean"/>
      <property Name="SoftwareElementID" IsArray="False" DataType="string"/>
      <property Name="SoftwareElementState" IsArray="False" DataType="uint16"/>
      <property Name="Status" IsArray="False" DataType="string"/>
      <property Name="TargetOperatingSystem" IsArray="False" DataType="uint16"/>
      <property Name="Version" IsArray="False" DataType="string"/>
    </properties>
  </data>

GETTING STARTED

Whether you are using Visual Studio 2010 or higher, the first thing you're going to want to do is create a new Windows Application project in C#.Net. The second thing you're going to need to do is make a few references:

From the list of .Net namespaces:

ADODB
Microsoft.Office.Interop.Excel

From the list of .COM namespaces:
Microsoft WMI Scripting v1.2 Library
Microsoft Scripting Runtime
Microsoft Shell Controls and Automation

```
using System;
using System.Collections.Generic;
using System.Linq;
using System.Text;
using WbemScripting;
using ADODB;
using Scripting;
using Shell32;
using Microsoft.Office.Interop;
namespace WindowsFormsApplication5
{
    class Class2
    {
```

DECLARING VARIABLES

As you can see from the below code, we are enabling the use of specific variables and objects at the very top of the module ns is made public so that the form can specify what WMI namespace will be used by the program along with what class will be called upon to provide us with information about your local machine. The old school version of the FileSystem Object is created along with an empty object we're going to be using as the textstream.

```
Dictionary<Int32, string> Names = new Dictionary<Int32,
string>();
Dictionary<Int32, Dictionary<Int32, string>> Rows = new
Dictionary<Int32, Dictionary<Int32, string>>();
String Orientation = "Multi-Line Horizontal";
int x = 0;
int y = 0;
SWbemSink Sink = null;
```

THE INITIALIZATION CODE

The purpose of this function is to return a collection of objects and properties we can use to populate and view in a variety of formats and orientations.

```
public void Initialize()
  {

        WbemScripting.SWbemLocator l = new SWbemLocator();
        WbemScripting.SWbemServices svc =
l.ConnectServer(".", "root\\cimv2");
        svc.Security_.AuthenticationLevel =
WbemAuthenticationLevelEnum.wbemAuthenticationLevelPktPrivacy;
        svc.Security_.ImpersonationLevel =
WbemImpersonationLevelEnum.wbemImpersonationLevelImpersonate;
        Sink = new SWbemSink();
        Sink.OnCompleted += new
ISWbemSinkEvents_OnCompletedEventHandler(Sink_OnCompleted);
        Sink.OnObjectReady += new
ISWbemSinkEvents_OnObjectReadyEventHandler(Sink_OnObjectReady);
        svc.ExecNotificationQueryAsync(Sink, "Select * From
__InstanceOperationEvent within 1 Where targetInstance ISA
'Win32_Process'");
        }


        private void Sink_OnCompleted(WbemScripting.WbemErrorEnum
iHResult, WbemScripting.SWbemObject objWbemErrorObject,
WbemScripting.SWbemNamedValueSet objWbemAsyncContext)
        {

        Create_HTML_Code();

        }
```

```csharp
        private void Sink_OnObjectReady(SWbemObject
objWbemObject, SWbemNamedValueSet objWbemAsyncContext)
        {

            if (y == 1)
            {
                Sink.Cancel();
                Create_HTML_Code();
                return;
            }



            SWbemObject obj =
objWbemObject.Properties_.Item("TargetInstance").get_Value();

            if (y == 0)
            {
                foreach (SWbemProperty prop in obj.Properties_)
                {
                    Names[x] = prop.Name;
                    x = x + 1;
                }
                x = 0;
            }

            Dictionary<Int32, string> Cols = new
Dictionary<Int32, string>();
            foreach (SWbemProperty prop in obj.Properties_)
            {
                Cols[x] = GetValue(prop.Name, obj);
                x = x + 1;
            }
            x = 0;
            Rows[y] = Cols;
            y = y + 1;

        }
```

CREATE ASP CODE

Inside this sub routine is the code to create an ASP Webpage.

```
private void Create_ASP_Code()
{

        Scripting.FileSystemObject fso = new Scripting.FileSystemObject();
        Scripting.TextStream                    txtstream                    =
fso.OpenTextFile(System.Environment.CurrentDirectory    +    "\\Process.asp",
Scripting.IOMode.ForWriting, true, Scripting.Tristate.TristateUseDefault);
        txtstream.WriteLine("<html
xmlns=\"http://www.w3.org/1999/xhtml\">");
        txtstream.WriteLine("<head>");
        txtstream.WriteLine("<title>Win32_Process</title>");
        txtstream.WriteLine("<style type='text/css'>");
        txtstream.WriteLine("body");
        txtstream.WriteLine("{");
        txtstream.WriteLine("    PADDING-RIGHT: 0px;");
        txtstream.WriteLine("    PADDING-LEFT: 0px;");
        txtstream.WriteLine("    PADDING-BOTTOM: 0px;");
        txtstream.WriteLine("    MARGIN: 0px;");
        txtstream.WriteLine("    COLOR: #333;");
        txtstream.WriteLine("    PADDING-TOP: 0px;");
        txtstream.WriteLine("    FONT-FAMILY: verdana, arial, helvetica, sans-
serif;");
        txtstream.WriteLine("}");
        txtstream.WriteLine("table");
        txtstream.WriteLine("{");
        txtstream.WriteLine("    BORDER-RIGHT: #999999 1px solid;");
```

```
txtstream.WriteLine("   PADDING-RIGHT: 1px;");
txtstream.WriteLine("   PADDING-LEFT: 1px;");
txtstream.WriteLine("   PADDING-BOTTOM: 1px;");
txtstream.WriteLine("   LINE-HEIGHT: 8px;");
txtstream.WriteLine("   PADDING-TOP: 1px;");
txtstream.WriteLine("   BORDER-BOTTOM: #999 1px solid;");
txtstream.WriteLine("   BACKGROUND-COLOR: #eeeeee;");
txtstream.WriteLine("
filter:progid:DXImageTransform.Microsoft.Shadow(color='silver',    Direction=135,
Strength=16)");
txtstream.WriteLine("}");
txtstream.WriteLine("th");
txtstream.WriteLine("{");
txtstream.WriteLine("   BORDER-RIGHT: #999999 3px solid;");
txtstream.WriteLine("   PADDING-RIGHT: 6px;");
txtstream.WriteLine("   PADDING-LEFT: 6px;");
txtstream.WriteLine("   FONT-WEIGHT: Bold;");
txtstream.WriteLine("   FONT-SIZE: 14px;");
txtstream.WriteLine("   PADDING-BOTTOM: 6px;");
txtstream.WriteLine("   COLOR: darkred;");
txtstream.WriteLine("   LINE-HEIGHT: 14px;");
txtstream.WriteLine("   PADDING-TOP: 6px;");
txtstream.WriteLine("   BORDER-BOTTOM: #999 1px solid;");
txtstream.WriteLine("   BACKGROUND-COLOR: #eeeeee;");
txtstream.WriteLine("   FONT-FAMILY: font-family: Cambria, serif;");
txtstream.WriteLine("   FONT-SIZE: 12px;");
txtstream.WriteLine("   text-align: left;");
txtstream.WriteLine("   white-Space: nowrap;");
txtstream.WriteLine("}");
txtstream.WriteLine(".th");
txtstream.WriteLine("{");
txtstream.WriteLine("   BORDER-RIGHT: #999999 2px solid;");
txtstream.WriteLine("   PADDING-RIGHT: 6px;");
```

```
txtstream.WriteLine("    PADDING-LEFT: 6px;");
txtstream.WriteLine("    FONT-WEIGHT: Bold;");
txtstream.WriteLine("    PADDING-BOTTOM: 6px;");
txtstream.WriteLine("    COLOR: black;");
txtstream.WriteLine("    PADDING-TOP: 6px;");
txtstream.WriteLine("    BORDER-BOTTOM: #999 2px solid;");
txtstream.WriteLine("    BACKGROUND-COLOR: #eeeeee;");
txtstream.WriteLine("    FONT-FAMILY: font-family: Cambria, serif;");
txtstream.WriteLine("    FONT-SIZE: 10px;");
txtstream.WriteLine("    text-align: right;");
txtstream.WriteLine("    white-Space: nowrap;");
txtstream.WriteLine("}");
txtstream.WriteLine("td");
txtstream.WriteLine("{");
txtstream.WriteLine("    BORDER-RIGHT: #999999 3px solid;");
txtstream.WriteLine("    PADDING-RIGHT: 6px;");
txtstream.WriteLine("    PADDING-LEFT: 6px;");
txtstream.WriteLine("    FONT-WEIGHT: Normal;");
txtstream.WriteLine("    PADDING-BOTTOM: 6px;");
txtstream.WriteLine("    COLOR: navy;");
txtstream.WriteLine("    LINE-HEIGHT: 14px;");
txtstream.WriteLine("    PADDING-TOP: 6px;");
txtstream.WriteLine("    BORDER-BOTTOM: #999 1px solid;");
txtstream.WriteLine("    BACKGROUND-COLOR: #eeeeee;");
txtstream.WriteLine("    FONT-FAMILY: font-family: Cambria, serif;");
txtstream.WriteLine("    FONT-SIZE: 12px;");
txtstream.WriteLine("    text-align: left;");
txtstream.WriteLine("    white-Space: nowrap;");
txtstream.WriteLine("}");
txtstream.WriteLine("div");
txtstream.WriteLine("{");
txtstream.WriteLine("    BORDER-RIGHT: #999999 3px solid;");
txtstream.WriteLine("    PADDING-RIGHT: 6px;");
```

```
txtstream.WriteLine("    PADDING-LEFT: 6px;");
txtstream.WriteLine("    FONT-WEIGHT: Normal;");
txtstream.WriteLine("    PADDING-BOTTOM: 6px;");
txtstream.WriteLine("    COLOR: white;");
txtstream.WriteLine("    PADDING-TOP: 6px;");
txtstream.WriteLine("    BORDER-BOTTOM: #999 1px solid;");
txtstream.WriteLine("    BACKGROUND-COLOR: navy;");
txtstream.WriteLine("    FONT-FAMILY: font-family: Cambria, serif;");
txtstream.WriteLine("    FONT-SIZE: 10px;");
txtstream.WriteLine("    text-align: left;");
txtstream.WriteLine("    white-Space: nowrap;");
txtstream.WriteLine("}");
txtstream.WriteLine("span");
txtstream.WriteLine("{");
txtstream.WriteLine("    BORDER-RIGHT: #999999 3px solid;");
txtstream.WriteLine("    PADDING-RIGHT: 3px;");
txtstream.WriteLine("    PADDING-LEFT: 3px;");
txtstream.WriteLine("    FONT-WEIGHT: Normal;");
txtstream.WriteLine("    PADDING-BOTTOM: 3px;");
txtstream.WriteLine("    COLOR: white;");
txtstream.WriteLine("    PADDING-TOP: 3px;");
txtstream.WriteLine("    BORDER-BOTTOM: #999 1px solid;");
txtstream.WriteLine("    BACKGROUND-COLOR: navy;");
txtstream.WriteLine("    FONT-FAMILY: font-family: Cambria, serif;");
txtstream.WriteLine("    FONT-SIZE: 10px;");
txtstream.WriteLine("    text-align: left;");
txtstream.WriteLine("    white-Space: nowrap;");
txtstream.WriteLine("    display: inline-block;");
txtstream.WriteLine("    width: 100%;");
txtstream.WriteLine("}");
txtstream.WriteLine("textarea");
txtstream.WriteLine("{");
txtstream.WriteLine("    BORDER-RIGHT: #999999 3px solid;");
```

```
txtstream.WriteLine("    PADDING-RIGHT: 3px;");
txtstream.WriteLine("    PADDING-LEFT: 3px;");
txtstream.WriteLine("    FONT-WEIGHT: Normal;");
txtstream.WriteLine("    PADDING-BOTTOM: 3px;");
txtstream.WriteLine("    COLOR: white;");
txtstream.WriteLine("    PADDING-TOP: 3px;");
txtstream.WriteLine("    BORDER-BOTTOM: #999 1px solid;");
txtstream.WriteLine("    BACKGROUND-COLOR: navy;");
txtstream.WriteLine("    FONT-FAMILY: font-family: Cambria, serif;");
txtstream.WriteLine("    FONT-SIZE: 10px;");
txtstream.WriteLine("    text-align: left;");
txtstream.WriteLine("    white-Space: nowrap;");
txtstream.WriteLine("    width: 100%;");
txtstream.WriteLine("}");
txtstream.WriteLine("select");
txtstream.WriteLine("{");
txtstream.WriteLine("    BORDER-RIGHT: #999999 3px solid;");
txtstream.WriteLine("    PADDING-RIGHT: 6px;");
txtstream.WriteLine("    PADDING-LEFT: 6px;");
txtstream.WriteLine("    FONT-WEIGHT: Normal;");
txtstream.WriteLine("    PADDING-BOTTOM: 6px;");
txtstream.WriteLine("    COLOR: white;");
txtstream.WriteLine("    PADDING-TOP: 6px;");
txtstream.WriteLine("    BORDER-BOTTOM: #999 1px solid;");
txtstream.WriteLine("    BACKGROUND-COLOR: navy;");
txtstream.WriteLine("    FONT-FAMILY: font-family: Cambria, serif;");
txtstream.WriteLine("    FONT-SIZE: 10px;");
txtstream.WriteLine("    text-align: left;");
txtstream.WriteLine("    white-Space: nowrap;");
txtstream.WriteLine("    width: 100%;");
txtstream.WriteLine("}");
txtstream.WriteLine("input");
txtstream.WriteLine("{");
```

```
txtstream.WriteLine("    BORDER-RIGHT: #999999 3px solid;");
txtstream.WriteLine("    PADDING-RIGHT: 3px;");
txtstream.WriteLine("    PADDING-LEFT: 3px;");
txtstream.WriteLine("    FONT-WEIGHT: Bold;");
txtstream.WriteLine("    PADDING-BOTTOM: 3px;");
txtstream.WriteLine("    COLOR: white;");
txtstream.WriteLine("    PADDING-TOP: 3px;");
txtstream.WriteLine("    BORDER-BOTTOM: #999 1px solid;");
txtstream.WriteLine("    BACKGROUND-COLOR: navy;");
txtstream.WriteLine("    FONT-FAMILY: font-family: Cambria, serif;");
txtstream.WriteLine("    FONT-SIZE: 12px;");
txtstream.WriteLine("    text-align: left;");
txtstream.WriteLine("    display: table-cell;");
txtstream.WriteLine("    white-Space: nowrap;");
txtstream.WriteLine("    width: 100%;");
txtstream.WriteLine("}");
txtstream.WriteLine("h1 {");
txtstream.WriteLine("color: antiquewhite;");
txtstream.WriteLine("text-shadow: 1px 1px 1px black;");
txtstream.WriteLine("padding: 3px;");
txtstream.WriteLine("text-align: center;");
txtstream.WriteLine("box-shadow: inset 2px 2px 5px rgba(0,0,0,0.5),
inset -2px -2px 5px rgba(255,255,255,0.5)");
txtstream.WriteLine("}");
txtstream.WriteLine("</style>");
txtstream.WriteLine("</head>");
txtstream.WriteLine("<body>");
txtstream.WriteLine("<%");
txtstream.WriteLine("Response.Write(\"<table            Border='1'
cellpadding='1' cellspacing='1'>\" + vbcrlf)");


switch (Orientation)
```

```
                    {

            case "Single-Line Horizontal":
                {
                    for (int y = 0; y < Rows.Count; y++)
                    {
                        txtstream.WriteLine("Response.Write(\"<tr>\" + vbcrlf)");
                        for (int x = 0; x < Names.Count; x++)
                        {
                            txtstream.WriteLine("Response.Write(\"<th>" + Names[x]
+ "</th>\" + vbcrlf)");
                        }
                        txtstream.WriteLine("Response.Write(\"</tr>\" + vbcrlf)");
                        txtstream.WriteLine("Response.Write(\"<tr>\" + vbcrlf)");
                        for (int x = 0; x < Names.Count; x++)
                        {
                            String value = Rows[y][x];
                            txtstream.WriteLine("Response.Write(\"<td>" + value +
"</td>\" + vbcrlf)");
                        }
                        txtstream.WriteLine("Response.Write(\"</tr>\" + vbcrlf)");
                        break;
                    }
                    break;
                }

            case "Multi-Line Horizontal":
                {

                    for (int y = 0; y < Rows.Count; y++)
                    {
                        txtstream.WriteLine("Response.Write(\"<tr>\" + vbcrlf)");
```

```
                for (int x = 0; x < Names.Count; x++)
                {
                    txtstream.WriteLine("Response.Write(\"<th>" + Names[x]
+ "</th>\" + vbcrlf)");
                }
                txtstream.WriteLine("Response.Write(\"</tr>\" + vbcrlf)");
                break;
            }
            for (int y = 0; y < Rows.Count; y++)
            {
                txtstream.WriteLine("Response.Write(\"<tr>\" + vbcrlf)");
                for (int x = 0; x < Names.Count; x++)
                {
                    string value = Rows[y][x];
                    txtstream.WriteLine("Response.Write(\"<td>" + value +
"</td>\" + vbcrlf)");
                }
                txtstream.WriteLine("Response.Write(\"</tr>\" + vbcrlf)");
            }
            break;
        }
    case "Single-Line Vertical":
        {

            for (int y = 0; y < Rows.Count; y++)
            {

                for (int x = 0; x < Names.Count; x++)
                {
                    txtstream.WriteLine("Response.Write(\"<tr><th>"          +
Names[x] + "</th><td>" + Rows[y][x] + "</td></tr>\" + vbcrlf)");
                }
                break;
```

```csharp
                    }
                    break;
                }

            case "Multi-Line Vertical":
                {

                    for (int x = 0; x < Names.Count; x++)
                    {

                        txtstream.WriteLine("Response.Write(\"<tr><th>"                    +
Names[x] + "</th>\" + vbcrlf)");
                        for (int y = 0; y < Rows.Count; y++)
                        {
                            string value = Rows[y][x];
                            txtstream.WriteLine("Response.Write(\"<td>"   +   value   +
"</td>\" + vbcrlf)");
                        }
                        txtstream.WriteLine("Response.Write(\"</tr>\" + vbcrlf)");
                    }
                    break;
                }

        }
        txtstream.WriteLine("Response.Write(\"</table>\" + vbcrlf)");
        txtstream.WriteLine("%>");
        txtstream.WriteLine("</body>");
        txtstream.WriteLine("</html>");
        txtstream.Close();
    }
```

CREATE ASPX CODE

Inside this sub routine is the code to create an ASPX Webpage.

```
private void Create_ASPX_Code()
{

    Scripting.FileSystemObject fso = new Scripting.FileSystemObject();
    Scripting.TextStream txtstream = fso.OpenTextFile(System.Environment.CurrentDirectory + "\\Process.aspx", Scripting.IOMode.ForWriting, true, Scripting.Tristate.TristateUseDefault);
    txtstream.WriteLine("<!DOCTYPE html PUBLIC \"-//W3C//DTD XHTML 1.0 Transitional//EN\" \"http://www.w3.org/TR/xhtml1/DTD/xhtml1-transitional.dtd\">");
    txtstream.WriteLine("");
    txtstream.WriteLine("<html xmlns=\"http://www.w3.org/1999/xhtml\">");
    txtstream.WriteLine("<head>");
    txtstream.WriteLine("<title>Win32_Process</title>");
    txtstream.WriteLine("<style type='text/css'>");
    txtstream.WriteLine("body");
    txtstream.WriteLine("{");
    txtstream.WriteLine("    PADDING-RIGHT: 0px;");
    txtstream.WriteLine("    PADDING-LEFT: 0px;");
    txtstream.WriteLine("    PADDING-BOTTOM: 0px;");
    txtstream.WriteLine("    MARGIN: 0px;");
    txtstream.WriteLine("    COLOR: #333;");
    txtstream.WriteLine("    PADDING-TOP: 0px;");
```

```
txtstream.WriteLine("    FONT-FAMILY: verdana, arial, helvetica, sans-
serif;");
            txtstream.WriteLine("}");
            txtstream.WriteLine("table");
            txtstream.WriteLine("{");
            txtstream.WriteLine("    BORDER-RIGHT: #999999 1px solid;");
            txtstream.WriteLine("    PADDING-RIGHT: 1px;");
            txtstream.WriteLine("    PADDING-LEFT: 1px;");
            txtstream.WriteLine("    PADDING-BOTTOM: 1px;");
            txtstream.WriteLine("    LINE-HEIGHT: 8px;");
            txtstream.WriteLine("    PADDING-TOP: 1px;");
            txtstream.WriteLine("    BORDER-BOTTOM: #999 1px solid;");
            txtstream.WriteLine("    BACKGROUND-COLOR: #eeeeee;");
            txtstream.WriteLine("
filter:progid:DXImageTransform.Microsoft.Shadow(color='silver',    Direction=135,
Strength=16)");
            txtstream.WriteLine("}");
            txtstream.WriteLine("th");
            txtstream.WriteLine("{");
            txtstream.WriteLine("    BORDER-RIGHT: #999999 3px solid;");
            txtstream.WriteLine("    PADDING-RIGHT: 6px;");
            txtstream.WriteLine("    PADDING-LEFT: 6px;");
            txtstream.WriteLine("    FONT-WEIGHT: Bold;");
            txtstream.WriteLine("    FONT-SIZE: 14px;");
            txtstream.WriteLine("    PADDING-BOTTOM: 6px;");
            txtstream.WriteLine("    COLOR: darkred;");
            txtstream.WriteLine("    LINE-HEIGHT: 14px;");
            txtstream.WriteLine("    PADDING-TOP: 6px;");
            txtstream.WriteLine("    BORDER-BOTTOM: #999 1px solid;");
            txtstream.WriteLine("    BACKGROUND-COLOR: #eeeeee;");
            txtstream.WriteLine("    FONT-FAMILY: font-family: Cambria, serif;");
            txtstream.WriteLine("    FONT-SIZE: 12px;");
            txtstream.WriteLine("    text-align: left;");
```

```
txtstream.WriteLine("    white-Space: nowrap;");
txtstream.WriteLine("}");
txtstream.WriteLine(".th");
txtstream.WriteLine("{");
txtstream.WriteLine("    BORDER-RIGHT: #999999 2px solid;");
txtstream.WriteLine("    PADDING-RIGHT: 6px;");
txtstream.WriteLine("    PADDING-LEFT: 6px;");
txtstream.WriteLine("    FONT-WEIGHT: Bold;");
txtstream.WriteLine("    PADDING-BOTTOM: 6px;");
txtstream.WriteLine("    COLOR: black;");
txtstream.WriteLine("    PADDING-TOP: 6px;");
txtstream.WriteLine("    BORDER-BOTTOM: #999 2px solid;");
txtstream.WriteLine("    BACKGROUND-COLOR: #eeeeee;");
txtstream.WriteLine("    FONT-FAMILY: font-family: Cambria, serif;");
txtstream.WriteLine("    FONT-SIZE: 10px;");
txtstream.WriteLine("    text-align: right;");
txtstream.WriteLine("    white-Space: nowrap;");
txtstream.WriteLine("}");
txtstream.WriteLine("td");
txtstream.WriteLine("{");
txtstream.WriteLine("    BORDER-RIGHT: #999999 3px solid;");
txtstream.WriteLine("    PADDING-RIGHT: 6px;");
txtstream.WriteLine("    PADDING-LEFT: 6px;");
txtstream.WriteLine("    FONT-WEIGHT: Normal;");
txtstream.WriteLine("    PADDING-BOTTOM: 6px;");
txtstream.WriteLine("    COLOR: navy;");
txtstream.WriteLine("    LINE-HEIGHT: 14px;");
txtstream.WriteLine("    PADDING-TOP: 6px;");
txtstream.WriteLine("    BORDER-BOTTOM: #999 1px solid;");
txtstream.WriteLine("    BACKGROUND-COLOR: #eeeeee;");
txtstream.WriteLine("    FONT-FAMILY: font-family: Cambria, serif;");
txtstream.WriteLine("    FONT-SIZE: 12px;");
txtstream.WriteLine("    text-align: left;");
```

```
txtstream.WriteLine("    white-Space: nowrap;");
txtstream.WriteLine("}");
txtstream.WriteLine("div");
txtstream.WriteLine("{");
txtstream.WriteLine("    BORDER-RIGHT: #999999 3px solid;");
txtstream.WriteLine("    PADDING-RIGHT: 6px;");
txtstream.WriteLine("    PADDING-LEFT: 6px;");
txtstream.WriteLine("    FONT-WEIGHT: Normal;");
txtstream.WriteLine("    PADDING-BOTTOM: 6px;");
txtstream.WriteLine("    COLOR: white;");
txtstream.WriteLine("    PADDING-TOP: 6px;");
txtstream.WriteLine("    BORDER-BOTTOM: #999 1px solid;");
txtstream.WriteLine("    BACKGROUND-COLOR: navy;");
txtstream.WriteLine("    FONT-FAMILY: font-family: Cambria, serif;");
txtstream.WriteLine("    FONT-SIZE: 10px;");
txtstream.WriteLine("    text-align: left;");
txtstream.WriteLine("    white-Space: nowrap;");
txtstream.WriteLine("}");
txtstream.WriteLine("span");
txtstream.WriteLine("{");
txtstream.WriteLine("    BORDER-RIGHT: #999999 3px solid;");
txtstream.WriteLine("    PADDING-RIGHT: 3px;");
txtstream.WriteLine("    PADDING-LEFT: 3px;");
txtstream.WriteLine("    FONT-WEIGHT: Normal;");
txtstream.WriteLine("    PADDING-BOTTOM: 3px;");
txtstream.WriteLine("    COLOR: white;");
txtstream.WriteLine("    PADDING-TOP: 3px;");
txtstream.WriteLine("    BORDER-BOTTOM: #999 1px solid;");
txtstream.WriteLine("    BACKGROUND-COLOR: navy;");
txtstream.WriteLine("    FONT-FAMILY: font-family: Cambria, serif;");
txtstream.WriteLine("    FONT-SIZE: 10px;");
txtstream.WriteLine("    text-align: left;");
txtstream.WriteLine("    white-Space: nowrap;");
```

```
txtstream.WriteLine("    display: inline-block;");
txtstream.WriteLine("    width: 100%;");
txtstream.WriteLine("}");
txtstream.WriteLine("textarea");
txtstream.WriteLine("{");
txtstream.WriteLine("    BORDER-RIGHT: #999999 3px solid;");
txtstream.WriteLine("    PADDING-RIGHT: 3px;");
txtstream.WriteLine("    PADDING-LEFT: 3px;");
txtstream.WriteLine("    FONT-WEIGHT: Normal;");
txtstream.WriteLine("    PADDING-BOTTOM: 3px;");
txtstream.WriteLine("    COLOR: white;");
txtstream.WriteLine("    PADDING-TOP: 3px;");
txtstream.WriteLine("    BORDER-BOTTOM: #999 1px solid;");
txtstream.WriteLine("    BACKGROUND-COLOR: navy;");
txtstream.WriteLine("    FONT-FAMILY: font-family: Cambria, serif;");
txtstream.WriteLine("    FONT-SIZE: 10px;");
txtstream.WriteLine("    text-align: left;");
txtstream.WriteLine("    white-Space: nowrap;");
txtstream.WriteLine("    width: 100%;");
txtstream.WriteLine("}");
txtstream.WriteLine("select");
txtstream.WriteLine("{");
txtstream.WriteLine("    BORDER-RIGHT: #999999 3px solid;");
txtstream.WriteLine("    PADDING-RIGHT: 6px;");
txtstream.WriteLine("    PADDING-LEFT: 6px;");
txtstream.WriteLine("    FONT-WEIGHT: Normal;");
txtstream.WriteLine("    PADDING-BOTTOM: 6px;");
txtstream.WriteLine("    COLOR: white;");
txtstream.WriteLine("    PADDING-TOP: 6px;");
txtstream.WriteLine("    BORDER-BOTTOM: #999 1px solid;");
txtstream.WriteLine("    BACKGROUND-COLOR: navy;");
txtstream.WriteLine("    FONT-FAMILY: font-family: Cambria, serif;");
txtstream.WriteLine("    FONT-SIZE: 10px;");
```

```
txtstream.WriteLine("    text-align: left;");
txtstream.WriteLine("    white-Space: nowrap;");
txtstream.WriteLine("    width: 100%;");
txtstream.WriteLine("}");
txtstream.WriteLine("input");
txtstream.WriteLine("{");
txtstream.WriteLine("    BORDER-RIGHT: #999999 3px solid;");
txtstream.WriteLine("    PADDING-RIGHT: 3px;");
txtstream.WriteLine("    PADDING-LEFT: 3px;");
txtstream.WriteLine("    FONT-WEIGHT: Bold;");
txtstream.WriteLine("    PADDING-BOTTOM: 3px;");
txtstream.WriteLine("    COLOR: white;");
txtstream.WriteLine("    PADDING-TOP: 3px;");
txtstream.WriteLine("    BORDER-BOTTOM: #999 1px solid;");
txtstream.WriteLine("    BACKGROUND-COLOR: navy;");
txtstream.WriteLine("    FONT-FAMILY: font-family: Cambria, serif;");
txtstream.WriteLine("    FONT-SIZE: 12px;");
txtstream.WriteLine("    text-align: left;");
txtstream.WriteLine("    display: table-cell;");
txtstream.WriteLine("    white-Space: nowrap;");
txtstream.WriteLine("    width: 100%;");
txtstream.WriteLine("}");
txtstream.WriteLine("h1 {");
txtstream.WriteLine("color: antiquewhite;");
txtstream.WriteLine("text-shadow: 1px 1px 1px black;");
txtstream.WriteLine("padding: 3px;");
txtstream.WriteLine("text-align: center;");
txtstream.WriteLine("box-shadow: inset 2px 2px 5px rgba(0,0,0,0.5),
inset -2px -2px 5px rgba(255,255,255,0.5)");
txtstream.WriteLine("}");
txtstream.WriteLine("</style>");
txtstream.WriteLine("</head>");
txtstream.WriteLine("<body>");
```

```
txtstream.WriteLine("<%");
txtstream.WriteLine("Response.Write(\"<table                Border='1'
cellpadding='1' cellspacing='1'>\" + vbcrlf)");


switch (Orientation)
{


    case "Single-Line Horizontal":
        {
            for (int y = 0; y < Rows.Count; y++)
            {
            txtstream.WriteLine("Response.Write(\"<tr>\" + vbcrlf)");
            for (int x = 0; x < Names.Count; x++)
            {
                txtstream.WriteLine("Response.Write(\"<th>"  +  Names[x]
+ "</th>\" + vbcrlf)");
            }
            txtstream.WriteLine("Response.Write(\"</tr>\" + vbcrlf)");
            txtstream.WriteLine("Response.Write(\"<tr>\" + vbcrlf)");
            for (int x = 0; x < Names.Count; x++)
            {
                String value = Rows[y][x];
                txtstream.WriteLine("Response.Write(\"<td>"  +  value  +
"</td>\" + vbcrlf)");
            }
            txtstream.WriteLine("Response.Write(\"</tr>\" + vbcrlf)");
            break;
            }
            break;
        }
```

```csharp
case "Multi-Line Horizontal":
{

    for (int y = 0; y < Rows.Count; y++)
    {
        txtstream.WriteLine("Response.Write(\"<tr>\" + vbcrlf)");
        for (int x = 0; x < Names.Count; x++)
        {
            txtstream.WriteLine("Response.Write(\"<th>" + Names[x] + "</th>\" + vbcrlf)");
        }
        txtstream.WriteLine("Response.Write(\"</tr>\" + vbcrlf)");
        break;
    }
    for (int y = 0; y < Rows.Count; y++)
    {
        txtstream.WriteLine("Response.Write(\"<tr>\" + vbcrlf)");
        for (int x = 0; x < Names.Count; x++)
        {
            string value = Rows[y][x];
            txtstream.WriteLine("Response.Write(\"<td>" + value + "</td>\" + vbcrlf)");
        }
        txtstream.WriteLine("Response.Write(\"</tr>\" + vbcrlf)");
    }
    break;
}
case "Single-Line Vertical":
{

    for (int y = 0; y < Rows.Count; y++)
    {
```

```
                        for (int x = 0; x < Names.Count; x++)
                        {
                            txtstream.WriteLine("Response.Write(\"<tr><th>"                +
Names[x] + "</th><td>" + Rows[y][x] + "</td></tr>\" + vbcrlf)");
                        }
                        break;
                    }
                    break;
                }

            case "Multi-Line Vertical":
                {

                    for (int x = 0; x < Names.Count; x++)
                    {

                        txtstream.WriteLine("Response.Write(\"<tr><th>"                +
Names[x] + "</th>\" + vbcrlf)");
                        for (int y = 0; y < Rows.Count; y++)
                        {
                            string value = Rows[y][x];
                            txtstream.WriteLine("Response.Write(\"<td>"    +    value    +
"</td>\" + vbcrlf)");
                        }
                        txtstream.WriteLine("Response.Write(\"</tr>\" + vbcrlf)");
                    }
                    break;
                }

        }
        txtstream.WriteLine("Response.Write(\"</table>\" + vbcrlf)");
        txtstream.WriteLine("%>");
        txtstream.WriteLine("</body>");
```

```
        txtstream.WriteLine("</html>");
        txtstream.Close();
        txtstream.WriteLine("</body>");
        txtstream.WriteLine("</html>");
        txtstream.Close();
    }
```

CREATE HTA CODE

Inside this sub routine is the code to create an HTA Application.

```
private void Create_HTA_Code()
{

    Scripting.FileSystemObject fso = new Scripting.FileSystemObject();
    Scripting.TextStream                 txtstream                 =
fso.OpenTextFile(System.Environment.CurrentDirectory    +    "\\Process.hta",
Scripting.IOMode.ForWriting, true, Scripting.Tristate.TristateUseDefault);
    txtstream.WriteLine("<html>");
    txtstream.WriteLine("<head>");
    txtstream.WriteLine("<HTA:APPLICATION ");
    txtstream.WriteLine("ID = \"Process\" ");
    txtstream.WriteLine("APPLICATIONNAME = \"Process\" ");
    txtstream.WriteLine("SCROLL = \"yes\" ");
    txtstream.WriteLine("SINGLEINSTANCE = \"yes\" ");
    txtstream.WriteLine("WINDOWSTATE = \"maximize\" >");
    txtstream.WriteLine("<title>Win32_Process</title>");
    txtstream.WriteLine("<style type='text/css'>");
    txtstream.WriteLine("body");
    txtstream.WriteLine("{");
    txtstream.WriteLine("    PADDING-RIGHT: 0px;");
    txtstream.WriteLine("    PADDING-LEFT: 0px;");
    txtstream.WriteLine("    PADDING-BOTTOM: 0px;");
    txtstream.WriteLine("    MARGIN: 0px;");
    txtstream.WriteLine("    COLOR: #333;");
    txtstream.WriteLine("    PADDING-TOP: 0px;");
```

```
txtstream.WriteLine("    FONT-FAMILY: verdana, arial, helvetica, sans-
serif;");
        txtstream.WriteLine("}");
        txtstream.WriteLine("table");
        txtstream.WriteLine("{");
        txtstream.WriteLine("    BORDER-RIGHT: #999999 1px solid;");
        txtstream.WriteLine("    PADDING-RIGHT: 1px;");
        txtstream.WriteLine("    PADDING-LEFT: 1px;");
        txtstream.WriteLine("    PADDING-BOTTOM: 1px;");
        txtstream.WriteLine("    LINE-HEIGHT: 8px;");
        txtstream.WriteLine("    PADDING-TOP: 1px;");
        txtstream.WriteLine("    BORDER-BOTTOM: #999 1px solid;");
        txtstream.WriteLine("    BACKGROUND-COLOR: #eeeeee;");
        txtstream.WriteLine("
filter:progid:DXImageTransform.Microsoft.Shadow(color='silver',    Direction=135,
Strength=16)");
        txtstream.WriteLine("}");
        txtstream.WriteLine("th");
        txtstream.WriteLine("{");
        txtstream.WriteLine("    BORDER-RIGHT: #999999 3px solid;");
        txtstream.WriteLine("    PADDING-RIGHT: 6px;");
        txtstream.WriteLine("    PADDING-LEFT: 6px;");
        txtstream.WriteLine("    FONT-WEIGHT: Bold;");
        txtstream.WriteLine("    FONT-SIZE: 14px;");
        txtstream.WriteLine("    PADDING-BOTTOM: 6px;");
        txtstream.WriteLine("    COLOR: darkred;");
        txtstream.WriteLine("    LINE-HEIGHT: 14px;");
        txtstream.WriteLine("    PADDING-TOP: 6px;");
        txtstream.WriteLine("    BORDER-BOTTOM: #999 1px solid;");
        txtstream.WriteLine("    BACKGROUND-COLOR: #eeeeee;");
        txtstream.WriteLine("    FONT-FAMILY: font-family: Cambria, serif;");
        txtstream.WriteLine("    FONT-SIZE: 12px;");
        txtstream.WriteLine("    text-align: left;");
```

```
txtstream.WriteLine("    white-Space: nowrap;");
txtstream.WriteLine("}");
txtstream.WriteLine(".th");
txtstream.WriteLine("{");
txtstream.WriteLine("    BORDER-RIGHT: #999999 2px solid;");
txtstream.WriteLine("    PADDING-RIGHT: 6px;");
txtstream.WriteLine("    PADDING-LEFT: 6px;");
txtstream.WriteLine("    FONT-WEIGHT: Bold;");
txtstream.WriteLine("    PADDING-BOTTOM: 6px;");
txtstream.WriteLine("    COLOR: black;");
txtstream.WriteLine("    PADDING-TOP: 6px;");
txtstream.WriteLine("    BORDER-BOTTOM: #999 2px solid;");
txtstream.WriteLine("    BACKGROUND-COLOR: #eeeeee;");
txtstream.WriteLine("    FONT-FAMILY: font-family: Cambria, serif;");
txtstream.WriteLine("    FONT-SIZE: 10px;");
txtstream.WriteLine("    text-align: right;");
txtstream.WriteLine("    white-Space: nowrap;");
txtstream.WriteLine("}");
txtstream.WriteLine("td");
txtstream.WriteLine("{");
txtstream.WriteLine("    BORDER-RIGHT: #999999 3px solid;");
txtstream.WriteLine("    PADDING-RIGHT: 6px;");
txtstream.WriteLine("    PADDING-LEFT: 6px;");
txtstream.WriteLine("    FONT-WEIGHT: Normal;");
txtstream.WriteLine("    PADDING-BOTTOM: 6px;");
txtstream.WriteLine("    COLOR: navy;");
txtstream.WriteLine("    LINE-HEIGHT: 14px;");
txtstream.WriteLine("    PADDING-TOP: 6px;");
txtstream.WriteLine("    BORDER-BOTTOM: #999 1px solid;");
txtstream.WriteLine("    BACKGROUND-COLOR: #eeeeee;");
txtstream.WriteLine("    FONT-FAMILY: font-family: Cambria, serif;");
txtstream.WriteLine("    FONT-SIZE: 12px;");
txtstream.WriteLine("    text-align: left;");
```

```
txtstream.WriteLine("    white-Space: nowrap;");
txtstream.WriteLine("}");
txtstream.WriteLine("div");
txtstream.WriteLine("{");
txtstream.WriteLine("    BORDER-RIGHT: #999999 3px solid;");
txtstream.WriteLine("    PADDING-RIGHT: 6px;");
txtstream.WriteLine("    PADDING-LEFT: 6px;");
txtstream.WriteLine("    FONT-WEIGHT: Normal;");
txtstream.WriteLine("    PADDING-BOTTOM: 6px;");
txtstream.WriteLine("    COLOR: white;");
txtstream.WriteLine("    PADDING-TOP: 6px;");
txtstream.WriteLine("    BORDER-BOTTOM: #999 1px solid;");
txtstream.WriteLine("    BACKGROUND-COLOR: navy;");
txtstream.WriteLine("    FONT-FAMILY: font-family: Cambria, serif;");
txtstream.WriteLine("    FONT-SIZE: 10px;");
txtstream.WriteLine("    text-align: left;");
txtstream.WriteLine("    white-Space: nowrap;");
txtstream.WriteLine("}");
txtstream.WriteLine("span");
txtstream.WriteLine("{");
txtstream.WriteLine("    BORDER-RIGHT: #999999 3px solid;");
txtstream.WriteLine("    PADDING-RIGHT: 3px;");
txtstream.WriteLine("    PADDING-LEFT: 3px;");
txtstream.WriteLine("    FONT-WEIGHT: Normal;");
txtstream.WriteLine("    PADDING-BOTTOM: 3px;");
txtstream.WriteLine("    COLOR: white;");
txtstream.WriteLine("    PADDING-TOP: 3px;");
txtstream.WriteLine("    BORDER-BOTTOM: #999 1px solid;");
txtstream.WriteLine("    BACKGROUND-COLOR: navy;");
txtstream.WriteLine("    FONT-FAMILY: font-family: Cambria, serif;");
txtstream.WriteLine("    FONT-SIZE: 10px;");
txtstream.WriteLine("    text-align: left;");
txtstream.WriteLine("    white-Space: nowrap;");
```

```
txtstream.WriteLine("    display: inline-block;");
txtstream.WriteLine("    width: 100%;");
txtstream.WriteLine("}");
txtstream.WriteLine("textarea");
txtstream.WriteLine("{");
txtstream.WriteLine("    BORDER-RIGHT: #999999 3px solid;");
txtstream.WriteLine("    PADDING-RIGHT: 3px;");
txtstream.WriteLine("    PADDING-LEFT: 3px;");
txtstream.WriteLine("    FONT-WEIGHT: Normal;");
txtstream.WriteLine("    PADDING-BOTTOM: 3px;");
txtstream.WriteLine("    COLOR: white;");
txtstream.WriteLine("    PADDING-TOP: 3px;");
txtstream.WriteLine("    BORDER-BOTTOM: #999 1px solid;");
txtstream.WriteLine("    BACKGROUND-COLOR: navy;");
txtstream.WriteLine("    FONT-FAMILY: font-family: Cambria, serif;");
txtstream.WriteLine("    FONT-SIZE: 10px;");
txtstream.WriteLine("    text-align: left;");
txtstream.WriteLine("    white-Space: nowrap;");
txtstream.WriteLine("    width: 100%;");
txtstream.WriteLine("}");
txtstream.WriteLine("select");
txtstream.WriteLine("{");
txtstream.WriteLine("    BORDER-RIGHT: #999999 3px solid;");
txtstream.WriteLine("    PADDING-RIGHT: 6px;");
txtstream.WriteLine("    PADDING-LEFT: 6px;");
txtstream.WriteLine("    FONT-WEIGHT: Normal;");
txtstream.WriteLine("    PADDING-BOTTOM: 6px;");
txtstream.WriteLine("    COLOR: white;");
txtstream.WriteLine("    PADDING-TOP: 6px;");
txtstream.WriteLine("    BORDER-BOTTOM: #999 1px solid;");
txtstream.WriteLine("    BACKGROUND-COLOR: navy;");
txtstream.WriteLine("    FONT-FAMILY: font-family: Cambria, serif;");
txtstream.WriteLine("    FONT-SIZE: 10px;");
```

```
txtstream.WriteLine("    text-align: left;");
txtstream.WriteLine("    white-Space: nowrap;");
txtstream.WriteLine("    width: 100%;");
txtstream.WriteLine("}");
txtstream.WriteLine("input");
txtstream.WriteLine("{");
txtstream.WriteLine("    BORDER-RIGHT: #999999 3px solid;");
txtstream.WriteLine("    PADDING-RIGHT: 3px;");
txtstream.WriteLine("    PADDING-LEFT: 3px;");
txtstream.WriteLine("    FONT-WEIGHT: Bold;");
txtstream.WriteLine("    PADDING-BOTTOM: 3px;");
txtstream.WriteLine("    COLOR: white;");
txtstream.WriteLine("    PADDING-TOP: 3px;");
txtstream.WriteLine("    BORDER-BOTTOM: #999 1px solid;");
txtstream.WriteLine("    BACKGROUND-COLOR: navy;");
txtstream.WriteLine("    FONT-FAMILY: font-family: Cambria, serif;");
txtstream.WriteLine("    FONT-SIZE: 12px;");
txtstream.WriteLine("    text-align: left;");
txtstream.WriteLine("    display: table-cell;");
txtstream.WriteLine("    white-Space: nowrap;");
txtstream.WriteLine("    width: 100%;");
txtstream.WriteLine("}");
txtstream.WriteLine("h1 {");
txtstream.WriteLine("color: antiquewhite;");
txtstream.WriteLine("text-shadow: 1px 1px 1px black;");
txtstream.WriteLine("padding: 3px;");
txtstream.WriteLine("text-align: center;");
txtstream.WriteLine("box-shadow: inset 2px 2px 5px rgba(0,0,0,0.5),
inset -2px -2px 5px rgba(255,255,255,0.5)");
txtstream.WriteLine("}");
txtstream.WriteLine("</style>");
txtstream.WriteLine("</head>");
txtstream.WriteLine("<body>");
```

```csharp
txtstream.WriteLine("<table          Border='1'          cellpadding='1'
cellspacing='1'>");

switch (Orientation)
{


    case "Single-Line Horizontal":
        {
            for (int y = 0; y < Rows.Count; y++)
            {
                txtstream.WriteLine("<tr>");
                for (int x = 0; x < Names.Count; x++)
                {
                    txtstream.WriteLine("<th>" + Names[x] + "</th>");
                }
                txtstream.WriteLine("</tr>");
                txtstream.WriteLine("<tr>");
                for (int x = 0; x < Names.Count; x++)
                {
                    String value = Rows[y][x];
                    txtstream.WriteLine("<td>" + value + "</td>");
                }
                txtstream.WriteLine("</tr>");
                break;
            }
            break;
        }

    case "Multi-Line Horizontal":
        {
```

```csharp
            for (int y = 0; y < Rows.Count; y++)
            {
                txtstream.WriteLine("<tr>");
                for (int x = 0; x < Names.Count; x++)
                {
                    txtstream.WriteLine("<th>" + Names[x] + "</th>");
                }
                txtstream.WriteLine("</tr>");
                break;
            }
            for (int y = 0; y < Rows.Count; y++)
            {
                txtstream.WriteLine("<tr>");
                for (int x = 0; x < Names.Count; x++)
                {
                    string value = Rows[y][x];
                    txtstream.WriteLine("<td>" + value + "</td>");
                }
                txtstream.WriteLine("</tr>");
            }
            break;
        }
    case "Single-Line Vertical":
        {

            for (int y = 0; y < Rows.Count; y++)
            {

                for (int x = 0; x < Names.Count; x++)
                {
                    txtstream.WriteLine("<tr><th>" + Names[x] + "</th><td>"
+ Rows[y][x] + "</td></tr>");
                }
```

```
            break;
        }
        break;
    }

case "Multi-Line Vertical":
    {

        for (int x = 0; x < Names.Count; x++)
        {

            txtstream.WriteLine("<tr><th>" + Names[x] + "</th>");
            for (int y = 0; y < Rows.Count; y++)
            {
                string value = Rows[y][x];
                txtstream.WriteLine("<td>" + value + "</td>");
            }
            txtstream.WriteLine("</tr>");
        }
        break;
    }
}
txtstream.WriteLine("</table>");
txtstream.WriteLine("</body>");
txtstream.WriteLine("</html>");
txtstream.Close();
}
```

CREATE HTML CODE

Inside this sub routine is the code to create an HTML Webpage that can be saved and displayed using the Web Browser control or saved and displayed at a later time.

```
private void Create_HTML_Code()
{

    Scripting.FileSystemObject fso = new Scripting.FileSystemObject();
    Scripting.TextStream txtstream = fso.OpenTextFile(System.Environment.CurrentDirectory + "\\Process.html", Scripting.IOMode.ForWriting, true, Scripting.Tristate.TristateUseDefault);
        txtstream.WriteLine("<html>");
        txtstream.WriteLine("<head>");
        txtstream.WriteLine("<title>Win32_Process</title>");
        txtstream.WriteLine("<style type='text/css'>");
        txtstream.WriteLine("body");
        txtstream.WriteLine("{");
        txtstream.WriteLine("   PADDING-RIGHT: 0px;");
        txtstream.WriteLine("   PADDING-LEFT: 0px;");
        txtstream.WriteLine("   PADDING-BOTTOM: 0px;");
        txtstream.WriteLine("   MARGIN: 0px;");
        txtstream.WriteLine("   COLOR: #333;");
        txtstream.WriteLine("   PADDING-TOP: 0px;");
        txtstream.WriteLine("    FONT-FAMILY: verdana, arial, helvetica, sans-serif;");
        txtstream.WriteLine("}");
        txtstream.WriteLine("table");
        txtstream.WriteLine("{");
```

```
txtstream.WriteLine("    BORDER-RIGHT: #999999 1px solid;");
txtstream.WriteLine("    PADDING-RIGHT: 1px;");
txtstream.WriteLine("    PADDING-LEFT: 1px;");
txtstream.WriteLine("    PADDING-BOTTOM: 1px;");
txtstream.WriteLine("    LINE-HEIGHT: 8px;");
txtstream.WriteLine("    PADDING-TOP: 1px;");
txtstream.WriteLine("    BORDER-BOTTOM: #999 1px solid;");
txtstream.WriteLine("    BACKGROUND-COLOR: #eeeeee;");
txtstream.WriteLine("
filter:progid:DXImageTransform.Microsoft.Shadow(color='silver',      Direction=135,
Strength=16)");
txtstream.WriteLine("}");
txtstream.WriteLine("th");
txtstream.WriteLine("{");
txtstream.WriteLine("    BORDER-RIGHT: #999999 3px solid;");
txtstream.WriteLine("    PADDING-RIGHT: 6px;");
txtstream.WriteLine("    PADDING-LEFT: 6px;");
txtstream.WriteLine("    FONT-WEIGHT: Bold;");
txtstream.WriteLine("    FONT-SIZE: 14px;");
txtstream.WriteLine("    PADDING-BOTTOM: 6px;");
txtstream.WriteLine("    COLOR: darkred;");
txtstream.WriteLine("    LINE-HEIGHT: 14px;");
txtstream.WriteLine("    PADDING-TOP: 6px;");
txtstream.WriteLine("    BORDER-BOTTOM: #999 1px solid;");
txtstream.WriteLine("    BACKGROUND-COLOR: #eeeeee;");
txtstream.WriteLine("    FONT-FAMILY: font-family: Cambria, serif;");
txtstream.WriteLine("    FONT-SIZE: 12px;");
txtstream.WriteLine("    text-align: left;");
txtstream.WriteLine("    white-Space: nowrap;");
txtstream.WriteLine("}");
txtstream.WriteLine(".th");
txtstream.WriteLine("{");
txtstream.WriteLine("    BORDER-RIGHT: #999999 2px solid;");
```

```
txtstream.WriteLine("    PADDING-RIGHT: 6px;");
txtstream.WriteLine("    PADDING-LEFT: 6px;");
txtstream.WriteLine("    FONT-WEIGHT: Bold;");
txtstream.WriteLine("    PADDING-BOTTOM: 6px;");
txtstream.WriteLine("    COLOR: black;");
txtstream.WriteLine("    PADDING-TOP: 6px;");
txtstream.WriteLine("    BORDER-BOTTOM: #999 2px solid;");
txtstream.WriteLine("    BACKGROUND-COLOR: #eeeeee;");
txtstream.WriteLine("    FONT-FAMILY: font-family: Cambria, serif;");
txtstream.WriteLine("    FONT-SIZE: 10px;");
txtstream.WriteLine("    text-align: right;");
txtstream.WriteLine("    white-Space: nowrap;");
txtstream.WriteLine("}");
txtstream.WriteLine("td");
txtstream.WriteLine("{");
txtstream.WriteLine("    BORDER-RIGHT: #999999 3px solid;");
txtstream.WriteLine("    PADDING-RIGHT: 6px;");
txtstream.WriteLine("    PADDING-LEFT: 6px;");
txtstream.WriteLine("    FONT-WEIGHT: Normal;");
txtstream.WriteLine("    PADDING-BOTTOM: 6px;");
txtstream.WriteLine("    COLOR: navy;");
txtstream.WriteLine("    LINE-HEIGHT: 14px;");
txtstream.WriteLine("    PADDING-TOP: 6px;");
txtstream.WriteLine("    BORDER-BOTTOM: #999 1px solid;");
txtstream.WriteLine("    BACKGROUND-COLOR: #eeeeee;");
txtstream.WriteLine("    FONT-FAMILY: font-family: Cambria, serif;");
txtstream.WriteLine("    FONT-SIZE: 12px;");
txtstream.WriteLine("    text-align: left;");
txtstream.WriteLine("    white-Space: nowrap;");
txtstream.WriteLine("}");
txtstream.WriteLine("div");
txtstream.WriteLine("{");
txtstream.WriteLine("    BORDER-RIGHT: #999999 3px solid;");
```

```
txtstream.WriteLine("    PADDING-RIGHT: 6px;");
txtstream.WriteLine("    PADDING-LEFT: 6px;");
txtstream.WriteLine("    FONT-WEIGHT: Normal;");
txtstream.WriteLine("    PADDING-BOTTOM: 6px;");
txtstream.WriteLine("    COLOR: white;");
txtstream.WriteLine("    PADDING-TOP: 6px;");
txtstream.WriteLine("    BORDER-BOTTOM: #999 1px solid;");
txtstream.WriteLine("    BACKGROUND-COLOR: navy;");
txtstream.WriteLine("    FONT-FAMILY: font-family: Cambria, serif;");
txtstream.WriteLine("    FONT-SIZE: 10px;");
txtstream.WriteLine("    text-align: left;");
txtstream.WriteLine("    white-Space: nowrap;");
txtstream.WriteLine("}");
txtstream.WriteLine("span");
txtstream.WriteLine("{");
txtstream.WriteLine("    BORDER-RIGHT: #999999 3px solid;");
txtstream.WriteLine("    PADDING-RIGHT: 3px;");
txtstream.WriteLine("    PADDING-LEFT: 3px;");
txtstream.WriteLine("    FONT-WEIGHT: Normal;");
txtstream.WriteLine("    PADDING-BOTTOM: 3px;");
txtstream.WriteLine("    COLOR: white;");
txtstream.WriteLine("    PADDING-TOP: 3px;");
txtstream.WriteLine("    BORDER-BOTTOM: #999 1px solid;");
txtstream.WriteLine("    BACKGROUND-COLOR: navy;");
txtstream.WriteLine("    FONT-FAMILY: font-family: Cambria, serif;");
txtstream.WriteLine("    FONT-SIZE: 10px;");
txtstream.WriteLine("    text-align: left;");
txtstream.WriteLine("    white-Space: nowrap;");
txtstream.WriteLine("    display: inline-block;");
txtstream.WriteLine("    width: 100%;");
txtstream.WriteLine("}");
txtstream.WriteLine("textarea");
txtstream.WriteLine("{");
```

```
txtstream.WriteLine("    BORDER-RIGHT: #999999 3px solid;");
txtstream.WriteLine("    PADDING-RIGHT: 3px;");
txtstream.WriteLine("    PADDING-LEFT: 3px;");
txtstream.WriteLine("    FONT-WEIGHT: Normal;");
txtstream.WriteLine("    PADDING-BOTTOM: 3px;");
txtstream.WriteLine("    COLOR: white;");
txtstream.WriteLine("    PADDING-TOP: 3px;");
txtstream.WriteLine("    BORDER-BOTTOM: #999 1px solid;");
txtstream.WriteLine("    BACKGROUND-COLOR: navy;");
txtstream.WriteLine("    FONT-FAMILY: font-family: Cambria, serif;");
txtstream.WriteLine("    FONT-SIZE: 10px;");
txtstream.WriteLine("    text-align: left;");
txtstream.WriteLine("    white-Space: nowrap;");
txtstream.WriteLine("    width: 100%;");
txtstream.WriteLine("}");
txtstream.WriteLine("select");
txtstream.WriteLine("{");
txtstream.WriteLine("    BORDER-RIGHT: #999999 3px solid;");
txtstream.WriteLine("    PADDING-RIGHT: 6px;");
txtstream.WriteLine("    PADDING-LEFT: 6px;");
txtstream.WriteLine("    FONT-WEIGHT: Normal;");
txtstream.WriteLine("    PADDING-BOTTOM: 6px;");
txtstream.WriteLine("    COLOR: white;");
txtstream.WriteLine("    PADDING-TOP: 6px;");
txtstream.WriteLine("    BORDER-BOTTOM: #999 1px solid;");
txtstream.WriteLine("    BACKGROUND-COLOR: navy;");
txtstream.WriteLine("    FONT-FAMILY: font-family: Cambria, serif;");
txtstream.WriteLine("    FONT-SIZE: 10px;");
txtstream.WriteLine("    text-align: left;");
txtstream.WriteLine("    white-Space: nowrap;");
txtstream.WriteLine("    width: 100%;");
txtstream.WriteLine("}");
txtstream.WriteLine("input");
```

```
txtstream.WriteLine("{");
txtstream.WriteLine("    BORDER-RIGHT: #999999 3px solid;");
txtstream.WriteLine("    PADDING-RIGHT: 3px;");
txtstream.WriteLine("    PADDING-LEFT: 3px;");
txtstream.WriteLine("    FONT-WEIGHT: Bold;");
txtstream.WriteLine("    PADDING-BOTTOM: 3px;");
txtstream.WriteLine("    COLOR: white;");
txtstream.WriteLine("    PADDING-TOP: 3px;");
txtstream.WriteLine("    BORDER-BOTTOM: #999 1px solid;");
txtstream.WriteLine("    BACKGROUND-COLOR: navy;");
txtstream.WriteLine("    FONT-FAMILY: font-family: Cambria, serif;");
txtstream.WriteLine("    FONT-SIZE: 12px;");
txtstream.WriteLine("    text-align: left;");
txtstream.WriteLine("    display: table-cell;");
txtstream.WriteLine("    white-Space: nowrap;");
txtstream.WriteLine("    width: 100%;");
txtstream.WriteLine("}");
txtstream.WriteLine("h1 {");
txtstream.WriteLine("color: antiquewhite;");
txtstream.WriteLine("text-shadow: 1px 1px 1px black;");
txtstream.WriteLine("padding: 3px;");
txtstream.WriteLine("text-align: center;");
txtstream.WriteLine("box-shadow: inset 2px 2px 5px rgba(0,0,0,0.5), inset -2px -2px 5px rgba(255,255,255,0.5)");
txtstream.WriteLine("}");
txtstream.WriteLine("</style>");
txtstream.WriteLine("</head>");
txtstream.WriteLine("<body>");
txtstream.WriteLine("<table        Border='1'        cellpadding='1' cellspacing='1'>");


switch (Orientation)
```

```csharp
    {



        case "Single-Line Horizontal":
            {
                for (int y = 0; y < Rows.Count; y++)
                {
                    txtstream.WriteLine("<tr>");
                    for (int x = 0; x < Names.Count; x++)
                    {
                        txtstream.WriteLine("<th>" + Names[x] + "</th>");
                    }
                    txtstream.WriteLine("</tr>");
                    txtstream.WriteLine("<tr>");
                    for (int x = 0; x < Names.Count; x++)
                    {
                        String value = Rows[y][x];
                        txtstream.WriteLine("<td>" + value + "</td>");
                    }
                    txtstream.WriteLine("</tr>");
                    break;
                }
                break;
            }

        case "Multi-Line Horizontal":
            {

                for (int y = 0; y < Rows.Count; y++)
                {
                    txtstream.WriteLine("<tr>");
                    for (int x = 0; x < Names.Count; x++)
                    {
```

```
                    txtstream.WriteLine("<th>" + Names[x] + "</th>");
                }
                txtstream.WriteLine("</tr>");
                break;
            }
            for (int y = 0; y < Rows.Count; y++)
            {
                txtstream.WriteLine("<tr>");
                for (int x = 0; x < Names.Count; x++)
                {
                    string value = Rows[y][x];
                    txtstream.WriteLine("<td>" + value + "</td>");
                }
                txtstream.WriteLine("</tr>");
            }
            break;
        }
    case "Single-Line Vertical":
        {

            for (int y = 0; y < Rows.Count; y++)
            {

                for (int x = 0; x < Names.Count; x++)
                {
                    txtstream.WriteLine("<tr><th>" + Names[x] + "</th><td>"
+ Rows[y][x] + "</td></tr>");
                }
                break;
            }
            break;
        }
```

```
case "Multi-Line Vertical":
    {

        for (int x = 0; x < Names.Count; x++)
        {

            txtstream.WriteLine("<tr><th>" + Names[x] + "</th>");
            for (int y = 0; y < Rows.Count; y++)
            {
                string value = Rows[y][x];
                txtstream.WriteLine("<td>" + value + "</td>");
            }
            txtstream.WriteLine("</tr>");
        }
        break;
    }

}
txtstream.WriteLine("</table>");
txtstream.WriteLine("</body>");
txtstream.WriteLine("</html>");
txtstream.Close();
}
```

CREATE THE CSV FILE

Inside this sub routine is the code to create a CSV file. It is a separate routine because its extension -.csv – is seen by Excel – assuming it is installed as a text-based data file and knows what to do with it to display its contents.

```
String tempstr = "";
Scripting.FileSystemObject fso = new Scripting.FileSystemObject();
Scripting.TextStream                        txtstream                        =
fso.OpenTextFile(System.Environment.CurrentDirectory    +    "\\Process.csv",
Scripting.IOMode.ForWriting, true, Scripting.Tristate.TristateUseDefault);

switch (Orientation)
{

    case "Single-Line Horizontal":
      {

        for (int x = 0; x < Names.Count; x++)
        {
          if (tempstr != "")
          {
            tempstr = tempstr + ",";

          }
          tempstr = tempstr + Names[x];

        }
        txtstream.WriteLine(tempstr);
        tempstr = "";
```

```csharp
        for (int y = 0; y < Rows.Count; y++)
        {
            for (int x = 0; x < Names.Count; x++)
            {
                if (tempstr != "")
                {
                    tempstr = tempstr + ",";
                }
                tempstr = tempstr + '"' + Rows[y][x] + '"';

            }
            txtstream.WriteLine(tempstr);
            tempstr = "";

        }
        txtstream.Close();

        break;
    }
case "Vertical":
    {

        for (int x = 0; x < Names.Count; x++)
        {
            tempstr = Names[x];
            for (int y = 0; y < Rows.Count; y++)
            {

                if (tempstr != "")
                {
                    tempstr = tempstr + ",";
                }
```

```
                    tempstr = tempstr + (char)34 + Rows[y][x] + (char)34;

        }
        txtstream.WriteLine(tempstr);
        tempstr = "";
    }
    break;


    }
}


}
```

CREATE THE EXCEL FILE

Inside this sub routine is the code to create a CSV file and then open it using an older version of Excel.

```
String tempstr = "";
Scripting.FileSystemObject fso = new Scripting.FileSystemObject();
Scripting.TextStream                    txtstream                    =
fso.OpenTextFile(System.Environment.CurrentDirectory    +    "\\Process.csv",
Scripting.IOMode.ForWriting, true, Scripting.Tristate.TristateUseDefault);

switch (Orientation)
{

    case "Single-Line Horizontal":
      {

          for (int x = 0; x < Names.Count; x++)
          {
            if (tempstr != "")
            {
              tempstr = tempstr + ",";

            }
            tempstr = tempstr + Names[x];

          }
          txtstream.WriteLine(tempstr);
```

```csharp
                    tempstr = "";

                    for (int y = 0; y < Rows.Count; y++)
                    {
                        for (int x = 0; x < Names.Count; x++)
                        {
                            if (tempstr != "")
                            {
                                tempstr = tempstr + ",";
                            }
                            tempstr = tempstr + '"' + Rows[y][x] + '"';

                        }
                        txtstream.WriteLine(tempstr);
                        tempstr = "";

                    }
                    txtstream.Close();

                    break;
                }
            case "Vertical":
                {

                    for (int x = 0; x < Names.Count; x++)
                    {
                        tempstr = Names[x];
                        for (int y = 0; y < Rows.Count; y++)
                        {

                            if (tempstr != "")
                            {
                                tempstr = tempstr + ",";
```

```
                    }
                tempstr = tempstr + (char)34 + Rows[y][x] + (char)34;


              }
            txtstream.WriteLine(tempstr);
            tempstr = "";
          }
        break;


      }
    }


  }
```

EXCEL AUTOMATION CODE

Inside this sub routine is the code to create an instance of Excel and populate a worksheet. Both horizontal and vertical orientations are available, and the code automatically aligns and autofits the cells.

```
public void Do_Excel_Automation_Code()
{
    Microsoft.Office.Interop.Excel.Application oExcel = new Microsoft.Office.Interop.Excel.Application();
    Microsoft.Office.Interop.Excel.Workbook wb = oExcel.Workbooks.Add();
    Microsoft.Office.Interop.Excel.Worksheet ws = wb.Worksheets[0];
    switch (Orientation)
    {

        case "Horizontal":
            {
                for (int x = 0; x < Names.Count; x++)
                {
                    ws.Cells[1, x + 1] = Names[x];
                }
                for (int y = 0; y < Rows.Count; y++)
                {
                    for (int x = 0; x < Names.Count; x++)
                    {
                        ws.Cells[y + 2, x + 1] = Rows[y][x];
                    }
```

```csharp
                }
                break;
        }
        case "Vertical":
        {
            for (int x = 0; x < Names.Count; x++)
            {
                ws.Cells[x + 1, 1] = Names[x];
            }
            for (int y = 0; y < Rows.Count; y++)
            {
                for (int x = 0; x < Names.Count; x++)
                {
                    ws.Cells[x + 1, y + 2] = Rows[y][x];
                }
            }
            break;
        }
    }
    ws.Columns.HorizontalAlignment                                    =
Microsoft.Office.Interop.Excel.XlHAlign.xlHAlignLeft;
    ws.Columns.AutoFit();
}
public void Create_Text_File_Code()
{

    String tempstr = "";
    Scripting.FileSystemObject fso = new Scripting.FileSystemObject();
    Scripting.TextStream                    txtstream                 =
fso.OpenTextFile(System.Environment.CurrentDirectory      +      "\\Process.xml",
Scripting.IOMode.ForWriting, true, Scripting.Tristate.TristateUseDefault);

    switch (Orientation)
```

```
        {

    case "Single-Line Horizontal":
        {

            for (int x = 0; x < Names.Count; x++)
            {
                if (tempstr != "")
                {
                    tempstr = tempstr + Delim;

                }
                tempstr = tempstr + Names[x];

            }
            txtstream.WriteLine(tempstr);
            tempstr = "";

            for (int y = 0; y < Rows.Count; y++)
            {
                for (int x = 0; x < Names.Count; x++)
                {
                    if (tempstr != "")
                    {
                        tempstr = tempstr + Delim;
                    }
                    tempstr = tempstr + '"' + Rows[y][x] + '"';

                }
                txtstream.WriteLine(tempstr);
                tempstr = "";

            }
```

```
                    txtstream.Close();

                break;
            }
        case "Vertical":
            {

                for (int x = 0; x < Names.Count; x++)
                {
                    tempstr = Names[x];
                    for (int y = 0; y < Rows.Count; y++)
                    {

                        if (tempstr != "")
                        {
                            tempstr = tempstr + Delim;
                        }
                        tempstr = tempstr + (char)34 + Rows[y][x] + (char)34;

                    }
                    txtstream.WriteLine(tempstr);
                    tempstr = "";
                }
                break;

            }
        }

    }
```

CREATE CUSTOM

DELIMITED TEXT FILE

This sub routine is designed to provide you with maximum flexibility. You choose the orientation and the delimiter.

```
public void Create_Text_File_Code()
    {

        String tempstr = "";
        Scripting.FileSystemObject fso = new Scripting.FileSystemObject();
        Scripting.TextStream                    txtstream                    =
fso.OpenTextFile(System.Environment.CurrentDirectory      +      "\\Process.xml",
Scripting.IOMode.ForWriting, true, Scripting.Tristate.TristateUseDefault);

        switch (Orientation)
        {

            case "Single-Line Horizontal":
                {

                    for (int x = 0; x < Names.Count; x++)
                    {
```

```csharp
            if (tempstr != "")
            {
                tempstr = tempstr + Delim;

            }
            tempstr = tempstr + Names[x];

        }
        txtstream.WriteLine(tempstr);
        tempstr = "";

        for (int y = 0; y < Rows.Count; y++)
        {
            for (int x = 0; x < Names.Count; x++)
            {
                if (tempstr != "")
                {
                    tempstr = tempstr + Delim;
                }
                tempstr = tempstr + '"' + Rows[y][x] + '"';

            }
            txtstream.WriteLine(tempstr);
            tempstr = "";

        }
        txtstream.Close();

        break;
    }
case "Vertical":
    {
```

```
for (int x = 0; x < Names.Count; x++)
{
    tempstr = Names[x];
    for (int y = 0; y < Rows.Count; y++)
    {

        if (tempstr != "")
        {
            tempstr = tempstr + Delim;
        }
        tempstr = tempstr + (char)34 + Rows[y][x] + (char)34;

    }
    txtstream.WriteLine(tempstr);
    tempstr = "";
}
break;


        }
    }


}
```

CREATE AN EXCEL SPREADSHEET TEXT FILE

Simply put, this routine creates an Excel Spreadsheet File that will automatically be displayed by Excel as a worksheet.

```
public void Create_Excel_SpreadSheet()
{

    Scripting.FileSystemObject fso = new Scripting.FileSystemObject();
    Scripting.TextStream                        txtstream                        =
fso.OpenTextFile(System.Environment.CurrentDirectory        +        "\\Process.xml",
Scripting.IOMode.ForWriting, true, Scripting.Tristate.TristateUseDefault);
    txtstream.WriteLine("<?xml version='1.0'?>");
    txtstream.WriteLine("<?mso-application progid='Excel.Sheet'?>");
    txtstream.WriteLine("<Workbook        xmlns='urn:schemas-microsoft-
com:office:spreadsheet'        xmlns:o='urn:schemas-microsoft-com:office:office'
xmlns:x='urn:schemas-microsoft-com:office:excel'        xmlns:ss='urn:schemas-
microsoft-com:office:spreadsheet'        xmlns:html='http://www.w3.org/TR/REC-
html40'>");
    txtstream.WriteLine("    <Documentproperties xmlns='urn:schemas-
microsoft-com:office:office'>");
    txtstream.WriteLine("    <Author>Windows User</Author>");
    txtstream.WriteLine("    <LastAuthor>Windows User</LastAuthor>");
    txtstream.WriteLine("                    <Created>2007-11-
27T19:36:16Z</Created>");
    txtstream.WriteLine("    <Version>12.00</Version>");
    txtstream.WriteLine("    </Documentproperties>");
```

```
txtstream.WriteLine("          <ExcelWorkbook    xmlns='urn:schemas-
microsoft-com:office:excel'>");
txtstream.WriteLine("     <WindowHeight>11835</WindowHeight>");
txtstream.WriteLine("     <WindowWidth>18960</WindowWidth>");
txtstream.WriteLine("     <WindowTopX>120</WindowTopX>");
txtstream.WriteLine("     <WindowTopY>135</WindowTopY>");
txtstream.WriteLine("
<ProtectStructure>False</ProtectStructure>");
txtstream.WriteLine("
<ProtectWindows>False</ProtectWindows>");
txtstream.WriteLine("   </ExcelWorkbook>");
txtstream.WriteLine("   <Styles>");
txtstream.WriteLine("     <Style ss:ID='Default' ss:Name='Normal'>");
txtstream.WriteLine("        <Alignment ss:Vertical='Bottom'/>");
txtstream.WriteLine("        <Borders/>");
txtstream.WriteLine("                   <Font   ss:FontName='Calibri'
x:Family='Swiss' ss:Size='11' ss:Color='#000000'/>");
txtstream.WriteLine("        <Interior/>");
txtstream.WriteLine("        <NumberFormat/>");
txtstream.WriteLine("        <Protection/>");
txtstream.WriteLine("     </Style>");
txtstream.WriteLine("     <Style ss:ID='s62'>");
txtstream.WriteLine("        <Borders/>");
txtstream.WriteLine("                   <Font   ss:FontName='Calibri'
x:Family='Swiss' ss:Size='11' ss:Color='#000000' ss:Bold='1'/>");
txtstream.WriteLine("     </Style>");
txtstream.WriteLine("     <Style ss:ID='s63'>");
txtstream.WriteLine("                  <Alignment  ss:Horizontal='Left'
ss:Vertical='Bottom' ss:Indent='2'/>");
txtstream.WriteLine("                  <Font   ss:FontName='Verdana'
x:Family='Swiss' ss:Size='7.7' ss:Color='#000000'/>");
txtstream.WriteLine("     </Style>");
txtstream.WriteLine("   </Styles>");
```

```csharp
txtstream.WriteLine("<Worksheet ss:Name='Process'>");
txtstream.WriteLine("            <Table   x:FullColumns='1'   x:FullRows='1'
ss:DefaultRowHeight='24.9375'>");
txtstream.WriteLine("        <Column ss:AutoFitWidth='1' ss:Width='82.5'
ss:Span='5'/>");
txtstream.WriteLine("      <Row ss:AutoFitHeight='0'>");
for (int x = 0; x < Names.Count; x++)
{
    txtstream.WriteLine("                          <Cell   ss:StyleID='s62'><Data
ss:Type='String'>" + Names[x] + "</Data></Cell>");
}
txtstream.WriteLine("      </Row>");
for (int y = 0; y < Rows.Count; y++)
{
    txtstream.WriteLine("                      <Row     ss:AutoFitHeight='0'
ss:Height='13.5'>");
    for (int x = 0; x < Names.Count; x++)
    {
        txtstream.WriteLine("                              <Cell><Data
ss:Type='String'><![CDATA[" + Rows[y][x] + "]]></Data></Cell>");
    }
    txtstream.WriteLine("      </Row>");
}
txtstream.WriteLine("  </Table>");
txtstream.WriteLine("        <WorksheetOptions   xmlns='urn:schemas-
microsoft-com:office:excel'>");
txtstream.WriteLine("    <PageSetup>");
txtstream.WriteLine("      <Header x:Margin='0.3'/>");
txtstream.WriteLine("      <Footer x:Margin='0.3'/>");
txtstream.WriteLine("       <PageMargins x:Bottom='0.75' x:Left='0.7'
x:Right='0.7' x:Top='0.75'/>");
txtstream.WriteLine("    </PageSetup>");
txtstream.WriteLine("    <Unsynced/>");
```

```
            txtstream.WriteLine("     <Print>");
            txtstream.WriteLine("       <FitHeight>0</FitHeight>");
            txtstream.WriteLine("       <ValidPrinterInfo/>");
            txtstream.WriteLine("
<HorizontalResolution>600</HorizontalResolution>");
            txtstream.WriteLine("
<VerticalResolution>600</VerticalResolution>");
            txtstream.WriteLine("     </Print>");
            txtstream.WriteLine("    <Selected/>");
            txtstream.WriteLine("    <Panes>");
            txtstream.WriteLine("     <Pane>");
            txtstream.WriteLine("      <Number>3</Number>");
            txtstream.WriteLine("      <ActiveRow>9</ActiveRow>");
            txtstream.WriteLine("      <ActiveCol>7</ActiveCol>");
            txtstream.WriteLine("     </Pane>");
            txtstream.WriteLine("    </Panes>");
            txtstream.WriteLine("    <ProtectObjects>False</ProtectObjects>");
            txtstream.WriteLine("
<ProtectScenarios>False</ProtectScenarios>");
            txtstream.WriteLine("  </WorksheetOptions>");
            txtstream.WriteLine("</Worksheet>");
            txtstream.WriteLine("</Workbook>");
            txtstream.Close();

        }
```

CREATE AN XML FILE

This sub routine creates a very simple Element XML File. This file can be used with the MSDAOSP and therefore, becomes as database text file.

```
public void Create_Element_XML_Code()
{


    Scripting.FileSystemObject fso = new Scripting.FileSystemObject();
    Scripting.TextStream                    txtstream                    =
fso.OpenTextFile(System.Environment.CurrentDirectory    +    "\\Process.xml",
Scripting.IOMode.ForWriting, true, Scripting.Tristate.TristateUseDefault);
    txtstream.WriteLine("<?xml version='1.0' encoding='iso-8859-1'?>");
    txtstream.WriteLine("<data>");
    for (int y = 0; y < Rows.Count; y++)
    {
        txtstream.WriteLine("<Win32_process>");
        for (int x = 0; x < Names.Count; x++)
        {
            txtstream.WriteLine("<" + Names[x] + ">" + Rows[y][x] + "</" +
Names[x] + ">");
        }
        txtstream.WriteLine("</Win32_process>");
    }
    txtstream.WriteLine("</data>");
    txtstream.Close();


}
```

CREATE XML FOR XSL FILE

```
public void Create_Element_XML_For_XSL_Files_Code()
{

    Scripting.FileSystemObject fso = new Scripting.FileSystemObject();
    Scripting.TextStream                 txtstream                =
fso.OpenTextFile(System.Environment.CurrentDirectory     +     "\\Process.xml",
Scripting.IOMode.ForWriting, true, Scripting.Tristate.TristateUseDefault);
    txtstream.WriteLine("<?xml version='1.0' encoding='iso-8859-1'?>");
    txtstream.WriteLine("<?xml-stylesheet    type='Text/xsl'   href='"   +
System.Environment.CurrentDirectory + "\\Win32_Process.xsl'?>");
    txtstream.WriteLine("<data>");
    for (int y = 0; y < Rows.Count; y++)
    {
       txtstream.WriteLine("<Win32_process>");
       for (int x = 0; x < Names.Count; x++)
       {
          txtstream.WriteLine("<" + Names[x] + ">" + Rows[y][x] + "</" +
Names[x] + ">");
       }
       txtstream.WriteLine("</Win32_process>");
    }
    txtstream.WriteLine("</data>");
    txtstream.Close();

}
```

CREATE A SCHEMA XML

This sub routine creates a very simple Element XML File but is dependent upon the specified XSL file. It is opened by ADO and uses the MSDAOSP provider.

This file is then saved and can be used by the MSPERSIST provider.

```
public void Create_Schema_XML_Files_Code()
{

    Scripting.FileSystemObject fso = new Scripting.FileSystemObject();
    Scripting.TextStream                    txtstream                    =
fso.OpenTextFile(System.Environment.CurrentDirectory    +    "\\Process.xml",
Scripting.IOMode.ForWriting, true, Scripting.Tristate.TristateUseDefault);
    txtstream.WriteLine("<?xml version='1.0' encoding='iso-8859-1'?>");
    txtstream.WriteLine("<data>");
    for (int y = 0; y < Rows.Count; y++)
    {
        txtstream.WriteLine("<Win32_process>");
        for (int x = 0; x < Names.Count; x++)
        {
            txtstream.WriteLine("<" + Names[x] + ">" + Rows[y][x] + "</" +
Names[x] + ">");
        }
        txtstream.WriteLine("</Win32_process>");
    }
    txtstream.WriteLine("</data>");
    txtstream.Close();
```

```
ADODB.Recordset rs1 = new ADODB.Recordset();
rs1.ActiveConnection          =          "Provider=MSDAOSP;          Data
Source=msxml2.DSOControl";
rs1.Open(System.Environment.CurrentDirectory                      +
"\\Win32_Process.xml");


if          (fso.FileExists(System.Environment.CurrentDirectory          +
"\\Win32_Process_Schema.xml") == true)
    {
        fso.DeleteFile(System.Environment.CurrentDirectory          +
"\\Win32_Process_Schema.xml");
    }
rs1.Save(System.Environment.CurrentDirectory                      +
"\\Win32_Process_Schema.xml", PersistFormatEnum.adPersistXML);


    }
```

CREATE THE XSL FILES

Inside this sub routine is the code to create the XSL File designed to render the XML as an HTML Webpage. It can be saved and displayed using the Web Browser control or saved and displayed at a later time. Simply pass in the collection generated by the Return_Management_Collection and specify its orientation.

```
public void Create_XSL_Files_Code()
{

    Scripting.FileSystemObject fso = new Scripting.FileSystemObject();
    Scripting.TextStream                      txtstream                 =
fso.OpenTextFile(System.Environment.CurrentDirectory      +      "\\Process.xsl",
Scripting.IOMode.ForWriting, true, Scripting.Tristate.TristateUseDefault);

    switch (Orientation)
    {

        case "Single-Line Horizontal":
            {
                txtstream.WriteLine("<?xml    version='1.0'    encoding='UTF-
8'?>");
                txtstream.WriteLine("<xsl:stylesheet                version='1.0'
xmlns:xsl='http://www.w3.org/1999/XSL/Transform'>");
                txtstream.WriteLine("<xsl:template match=\"/\">");
                txtstream.WriteLine("<html>");
                txtstream.WriteLine("<head>");
                txtstream.WriteLine("<title>Products</title>");
```

```
txtstream.WriteLine("<style type='text/css'>");
txtstream.WriteLine("th");
txtstream.WriteLine("{");
txtstream.WriteLine("    COLOR: darkred;");
txtstream.WriteLine("    BACKGROUND-COLOR: white;");
txtstream.WriteLine("        FONT-FAMILY:font-family: Cambria, serif;");
txtstream.WriteLine("    FONT-SIZE: 12px;");
txtstream.WriteLine("    text-align: left;");
txtstream.WriteLine("    white-Space: nowrap;");
txtstream.WriteLine("}");
txtstream.WriteLine("td");
txtstream.WriteLine("{");
txtstream.WriteLine("    COLOR: navy;");
txtstream.WriteLine("    BACKGROUND-COLOR: white;");
txtstream.WriteLine("        FONT-FAMILY: font-family: Cambria, serif;");
txtstream.WriteLine("    FONT-SIZE: 12px;");
txtstream.WriteLine("    text-align: left;");
txtstream.WriteLine("    white-Space: nowrap;");
txtstream.WriteLine("}");
txtstream.WriteLine("</style>");
txtstream.WriteLine("</head>");
txtstream.WriteLine("<body bgcolor='#333333'>");
txtstream.WriteLine("<table colspacing='3' colpadding='3'>");
txtstream.WriteLine("<tr>");
for (int x = 0; x < Names.Count; x++)
{
    txtstream.WriteLine("<th>" + Names[x] + "</th>");
}
txtstream.WriteLine("</tr>");
txtstream.WriteLine("<tr>");
for (int x = 0; x < Names.Count; x++)
```

```
                    {
                        txtstream.WriteLine("<td><xsl:value-of
select=\"data/Win32_Process/" + Names[x] + "\"/></td>");
                    }
    .               txtstream.WriteLine("</tr>");
                    txtstream.WriteLine("</table>");
                    txtstream.WriteLine("</body>");
                    txtstream.WriteLine("</html>");
                    txtstream.WriteLine("</xsl:template>");
                    txtstream.WriteLine("</xsl:stylesheet>");
                    txtstream.Close();

                    break;
                }
            case "Multi Line Horizontal":
                {

                    txtstream.WriteLine("<?xml     version='1.0'     encoding='UTF-
8'?>");
                    txtstream.WriteLine("<xsl:stylesheet                 version='1.0'
xmlns:xsl='http://www.w3.org/1999/XSL/Transform'>");
                    txtstream.WriteLine("<xsl:template match=\"/\">");
                    txtstream.WriteLine("<html>");
                    txtstream.WriteLine("<head>");
                    txtstream.WriteLine("<title>Products</title>");
                    txtstream.WriteLine("<style type='text/css'>");
                    txtstream.WriteLine("th");
                    txtstream.WriteLine("{");
                    txtstream.WriteLine("    COLOR: darkred;");
                    txtstream.WriteLine("    BACKGROUND-COLOR: white;");
                    txtstream.WriteLine("      FONT-FAMILY:font-family: Cambria,
serif;");
                    txtstream.WriteLine("    FONT-SIZE: 12px;");
```

```
txtstream.WriteLine("    text-align: left;");
txtstream.WriteLine("    white-Space: nowrap;");
txtstream.WriteLine("}");
txtstream.WriteLine("td");
txtstream.WriteLine("{");
txtstream.WriteLine("    COLOR: navy;");
txtstream.WriteLine("    BACKGROUND-COLOR: white;");
txtstream.WriteLine("    FONT-FAMILY: font-family: Cambria, serif;");
txtstream.WriteLine("    FONT-SIZE: 12px;");
txtstream.WriteLine("    text-align: left;");
txtstream.WriteLine("    white-Space: nowrap;");
txtstream.WriteLine("}");
txtstream.WriteLine("</style>");
txtstream.WriteLine("</head>");
txtstream.WriteLine("<body bgcolor='#333333'>");
txtstream.WriteLine("<table colspacing='3' colpadding='3'>");
txtstream.WriteLine("<tr>");
for (int x = 0; x < Names.Count; x++)
{
    txtstream.WriteLine("<th>" + Names[x] + "</th>");
}
txtstream.WriteLine("</tr>");
txtstream.WriteLine("<xsl:for-each select=\"data/Win32_Process\">");
txtstream.WriteLine("<tr>");
for (int x = 0; x < Names.Count; x++)
{
    txtstream.WriteLine("<td><xsl:value-of select=\"data/Win32_Process/" + Names[x] + "\"/></td>");
}
txtstream.WriteLine("</tr>");
txtstream.WriteLine("</xsl:for-each>");
```

```
                    txtstream.WriteLine("</table>");
                    txtstream.WriteLine("</body>");
                    txtstream.WriteLine("</html>");
                    txtstream.WriteLine("</xsl:template>");
                    txtstream.WriteLine("</xsl:stylesheet>");
                    txtstream.Close();

                    break;
                }
            case "Single Line Vertical":
                {
                    txtstream.WriteLine("<?xml     version='1.0'     encoding='UTF-
8'?>");
                    txtstream.WriteLine("<xsl:stylesheet                    version='1.0'
xmlns:xsl='http://www.w3.org/1999/XSL/Transform'>");
                    txtstream.WriteLine("<xsl:template match=\"/\">");
                    txtstream.WriteLine("<html>");
                    txtstream.WriteLine("<head>");
                    txtstream.WriteLine("<title>Products</title>");
                    txtstream.WriteLine("<style type='text/css'>");
                    txtstream.WriteLine("th");
                    txtstream.WriteLine("{");
                    txtstream.WriteLine("   COLOR: darkred;");
                    txtstream.WriteLine("   BACKGROUND-COLOR: white;");
                    txtstream.WriteLine("      FONT-FAMILY:font-family: Cambria,
serif;");
                    txtstream.WriteLine("   FONT-SIZE: 12px;");
                    txtstream.WriteLine("   text-align: left;");
                    txtstream.WriteLine("   white-Space: nowrap;");
                    txtstream.WriteLine("}");
                    txtstream.WriteLine("td");
                    txtstream.WriteLine("{");
                    txtstream.WriteLine("   COLOR: navy;");
```

```
                    txtstream.WriteLine("    BACKGROUND-COLOR: white;");
                    txtstream.WriteLine("     FONT-FAMILY: font-family: Cambria,
serif;");

                    txtstream.WriteLine("    FONT-SIZE: 12px;");
                    txtstream.WriteLine("    text-align: left;");
                    txtstream.WriteLine("    white-Space: nowrap;");
                    txtstream.WriteLine("}");
                    txtstream.WriteLine("</style>");
                    txtstream.WriteLine("</head>");
                    txtstream.WriteLine("<body bgcolor='#333333'>");
                    txtstream.WriteLine("<table colspacing='3' colpadding='3'>");
                    for (int x = 0; x < Names.Count; x++)
                    {
                        txtstream.WriteLine("<tr><th>" + Names[x] + "</th>");
                        txtstream.WriteLine("<td><xsl:value-of
select=\"data/Win32_Process/" + Names[x] + "\"/></td></tr>");
                    }
                    txtstream.WriteLine("</table>");
                    txtstream.WriteLine("</body>");
                    txtstream.WriteLine("</html>");
                    txtstream.WriteLine("</xsl:template>");
                    txtstream.WriteLine("</xsl:stylesheet>");
                    txtstream.Close();

                    break;

                }
            case "Multi Line Vertical":
                {

                    txtstream.WriteLine("<?xml    version='1.0'    encoding='UTF-
8'?>");
```

```
txtstream.WriteLine("<xsl:stylesheet                    version='1.0'
xmlns:xsl='http://www.w3.org/1999/XSL/Transform'>");
txtstream.WriteLine("<xsl:template match=\"/\">");
txtstream.WriteLine("<html>");
txtstream.WriteLine("<head>");
txtstream.WriteLine("<title>Products</title>");
txtstream.WriteLine("<style type='text/css'>");
txtstream.WriteLine("th");
txtstream.WriteLine("{");
txtstream.WriteLine("    COLOR: darkred;");
txtstream.WriteLine("    BACKGROUND-COLOR: white;");
txtstream.WriteLine("        FONT-FAMILY:font-family: Cambria,
serif;");
txtstream.WriteLine("    FONT-SIZE: 12px;");
txtstream.WriteLine("    text-align: left;");
txtstream.WriteLine("    white-Space: nowrap;");
txtstream.WriteLine("}");
txtstream.WriteLine("td");
txtstream.WriteLine("{");
txtstream.WriteLine("    COLOR: navy;");
txtstream.WriteLine("    BACKGROUND-COLOR: white;");
txtstream.WriteLine("        FONT-FAMILY: font-family: Cambria,
serif;");
txtstream.WriteLine("    FONT-SIZE: 12px;");
txtstream.WriteLine("    text-align: left;");
txtstream.WriteLine("    white-Space: nowrap;");
txtstream.WriteLine("}");
txtstream.WriteLine("</style>");
txtstream.WriteLine("</head>");
txtstream.WriteLine("<body bgcolor='#333333'>");
txtstream.WriteLine("<table colspacing='3' colpadding='3'>");
for (int x = 0; x < Names.Count; x++)
{
```

```
                    txtstream.WriteLine("<tr><th>" + Names[x] + "</th>");
                    txtstream.WriteLine("<td><xsl:for-each
select=\"data/Win32_Process\">");
                    txtstream.WriteLine("<xsl:value-of  select=\"" + Names[x] +
"\"/></td>");

                    txtstream.WriteLine("</xsl:for-each></tr>");
                }
                txtstream.WriteLine("</table>");
                txtstream.WriteLine("</body>");
                txtstream.WriteLine("</html>");
                txtstream.WriteLine("</xsl:template>");
                txtstream.WriteLine("</xsl:stylesheet>");
                txtstream.Close();

                break;
            }
        }

    }
```

THE GETVALUE

FUNCTION

This is where a function called GetValue is the very first routine of the module and is used to return the value of the property in the row of an object collection. One of the first things I learned early on is that it is much easier to parse a string than to have to deal with converting a laundry list of property datatypes and react to the common datetime datatype. Either there is a value assigned to the Property or there isn't. Either that value is a datetime datatype or it isn't.

```csharp
        private string GetValue(string N,
WbemScripting.SWbemObject obj)
        {
            int pos = 0;
            string tN = N;
            string tempstr = obj.GetObjectText_(0);
            tN = tN + " = ";
            pos = tempstr.IndexOf(tN);
            if (pos > 0)
            {
                pos = pos + tN.Length;
                tempstr = tempstr.Substring(pos, tempstr.Length -
pos);
                pos = tempstr.IndexOf(";");
                tempstr = tempstr.Substring(0, pos);
                tempstr = tempstr.Replace("{", "");
                tempstr = tempstr.Replace("}", "");
                tempstr = tempstr.Replace("\"", "");
                tempstr = tempstr.Trim();
                if (obj.Properties_.Item(N).CIMType ==
WbemCimtypeEnum.wbemCimtypeDatetime && tempstr.Length > 14)
                {
```

```
                return ReturnDateTime(tempstr);
            }
            else
            {
                return tempstr;
            }
        }
        else
        {
            return "";
        }
    }
    private string ReturnDateTime(string Value)
    {
        return Value.Substring(4, 2) + "/" +
Value.Substring(6, 2) + "/" + Value.Substring(0, 4) + " " +
Value.Substring(8, 2) + ":" + Value.Substring(10, 2) + ":" +
Value.Substring(12, 2);
    }
  }
}
```

Stylesheets

The difference between boring and oh, wow!

The stylesheets in Appendix A, were used to render these pages. If you find one you like, feel free to use it.

Report:

Table

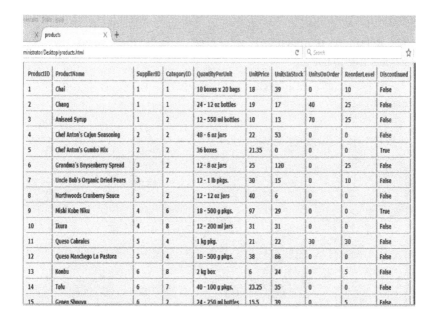

ProductID	ProductName	SupplierID	CategoryID	QuantityPerUnit	UnitPrice	UnitsInStock	UnitsOnOrder	ReorderLevel	Discontinued
1	Chai	1	1	10 boxes x 20 bags	18	39	0	10	False
2	Chang	1	1	24 - 12 oz bottles	19	17	40	25	False
3	Aniseed Syrup	1	2	12 - 550 ml bottles	10	13	70	25	False
4	Chef Anton's Cajun Seasoning	2	2	48 - 6 oz jars	22	53	0	0	False
5	Chef Anton's Gumbo Mix	2	2	36 boxes	21.35	0	0	0	True
6	Grandma's Boysenberry Spread	3	2	12 - 8 oz jars	25	120	0	25	False
7	Uncle Bob's Organic Dried Pears	3	7	12 - 1 lb pkgs.	30	15	0	10	False
8	Northwoods Cranberry Sauce	3	2	12 - 12 oz jars	40	6	0	0	False
9	Mishi Kobe Niku	4	6	18 - 500 g pkgs.	97	29	0	0	True
10	Ikura	4	8	12 - 200 ml jars	31	31	0	0	False
11	Queso Cabrales	5	4	1 kg pkg.	21	22	30	30	False
12	Queso Manchego La Pastora	5	4	10 - 500 g pkgs.	38	86	0	0	False
13	Konbu	6	8	2 kg box	6	24	0	5	False
14	Tofu	6	7	40 - 100 g pkgs.	23.25	35	0	0	False
15	Genen Shouyu	6	2	24 - 250 ml bottles	15.5	39	0	5	False

None:

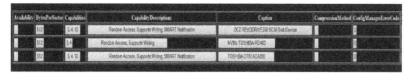

Black and White

Colored:

AccountExpires	AuthorizationFlags	BadPasswordCount	Caption	CodePage	Comment	CountryCode	Description
			NT AUTHORITY\SYSTEM				Network login profile settings for SYSTEM on NT AUTHORITY
			NT AUTHORITY\LOCAL SERVICE				Network login profile settings for LOCAL SERVICE on NT AUTHORITY
			NT AUTHORITY\NETWORK SERVICE				Network login profile settings for NETWORK SERVICE on NT AUTHORITY
	0	0	Administrator	0	Built-in account for administering the computer/domain	0	Network login profile settings for on WIN-AJRLOAKMJYH
			NT SERVICE\SSASTELEMETRY				Network login profile settings for SSASTELEMETRY on NT SERVICE
			NT SERVICE\SSISTELEMETRY130				Network login profile settings for SSISTELEMETRY130 on NT SERVICE
			NT SERVICE\SQLTELEMETRY				Network login profile settings for SQLTELEMETRY on NT SERVICE
			NT SERVICE\MSSQLServerOLAPService				Network login profile settings for MSSQLServerOLAPService on NT SERVICE
			NT SERVICE\ReportServer				Network login profile settings for ReportServer on NT SERVICE
			NT SERVICE\MSSQLFDLauncher				Network login profile settings for MSSQLFDLauncher on NT SERVICE
			NT SERVICE\MSSQLLaunchpad				Network login profile settings for MSSQLLaunchpad on NT SERVICE
			NT SERVICE\SdkDriver130				Network login profile settings for SdkDriver130 on NT SERVICE
			NT SERVICE\MSSQLSERVER				Network login profile settings for MSSQLSERVER on NT SERVICE
			IIS APPPOOL\Classic .NET AppPool				Network login profile settings for Classic .NET AppPool on IIS APPPOOL
			IIS APPPOOL\.NET v4.5				Network login profile settings for .NET v4.5 on IIS APPPOOL
			IIS APPPOOL\.NET v2.0				Network login profile settings for .NET v2.0 on IIS APPPOOL
			IIS APPPOOL\.NET v4.5 Classic				Network login profile settings for .NET v4.5 Classic on IIS APPPOOL
			IIS APPPOOL\.NET v2.0 Classic				Network login profile settings for .NET v2.0 Classic on IIS APPPOOL

Oscillating:

Availability	BytesPerSector	Capabilities	CapabilityDescriptions	Caption	CompressionMethod	ConfigManagerErrorCode	ConfigManagerUserConfig
	512	3, 4, 10	Random Access, Supports Writing, SMART Notification	OCZ REVODRIVE350 SCSI Disk Device		0	FALSE
	512	3, 4	Random Access, Supports Writing	NVMe TOSHIBA-RD400		0	FALSE
	512	3, 4, 10	Random Access, Supports Writing, SMART Notification	TOSHIBA DT01ACA200		0	FALSE

3D:

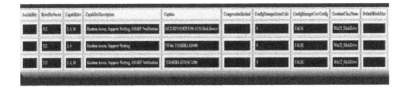

Availability	BytesPerSector	Capabilities	CapabilityDescriptions	Caption	CompressionMethod	ConfigManagerErrorCode	ConfigManagerUserConfig	CreationClassName
	512	3, 4, 10	Random Access, Supports Writing, SMART Notification	OCZ REVODRIVE350 SCSI Disk Device		0	FALSE	Win32_DiskDrive
	512	3, 4	Random Access, Supports Writing	NVMe TOSHIBA-RD400		0	FALSE	Win32_DiskDrive
	512	3, 4, 10	Random Access, Supports Writing, SMART Notification	TOSHIBA DT01ACA200		0	FALSE	Win32_DiskDrive

Shadow Box:

Availability	BytesPerSector	Capabilities	CapabilityDescriptions	Caption	CompressionMethod	ConfigManagerErrorCode	ConfigManagerUserConfig	CreationClassName	DefaultBlockSize
	512	3, 4, 10	Random Access, Supports Writing, SMART Notification	OCZ REVODRIVE350 SCSI Disk Device		0	FALSE	Win32_DiskDrive	
	512	3, 4	Random Access, Supports Writing	NVMe TOSHIBA-RD400		0	FALSE	Win32_DiskDrive	
	512	3, 4, 10	Random Access, Supports Writing, SMART Notification	TOSHIBA DT01ACA200		0	FALSE	Win32_DiskDrive	

89

Shadow Box Single Line Vertical

BiosCharacteristics	7, 10, 11, 12, 15, 16, 17, 19, 23, 24, 25, 26, 27, 28, 29, 32, 33, 40, 42, 43, 48, 50, 58, 59, 64, 65, 66, 67, 68, 69, 70, 71, 72, 73, 74, 75, 76, 77, 78, 79
BIOSVersion	ALASKA - 1072009, 0504, American Megatrends - 5000C
BuildNumber	
Caption	0504
CodeSet	
CurrentLanguage	en|US|iso8859-1
Description	0504
IdentificationCode	
InstallableLanguages	3
InstallDate	
LanguageEdition	
ListOfLanguages	en|US|iso8859-1, fr|FR|iso8859-1, zh|CN|unicode,,,,,
Manufacturer	American Megatrends Inc.
Name	0504
OtherTargetOS	
PrimaryBIOS	TRUE

Shadow Box Multi line Vertical

90

Availability			
BytesPerSector	512	512	512
Capabilities	3, 4, 10	3, 4	3, 4, 10
CapabilityDescriptions	Random Access, Supports Writing, SMART Notification	Random Access, Supports Writing	Random Access, Supports Writing, SMART Notification
Caption	OCZ REVODRIVE350 SCSI Disk Device	NVMe TOSHIBA-RD40	TOSHIBA DT01ACA300
CompressionMethod			
ConfigManagerErrorCode	0	0	0
ConfigManagerUserConfig	FALSE	FALSE	FALSE
CreationClassName	Win32_DiskDrive	Win32_DiskDrive	Win32_DiskDrive
DefaultBlockSize			
Description	Disk drive	Disk drive	Disk drive
DeviceID	\\.\PHYSICALDRIVE2	\\.\PHYSICALDRIVE1	\\.\PHYSICALDRIVE0
ErrorCleared			
ErrorDescription			
ErrorMethodology			
FirmwareRevision	2.50	57C7A102	MX4OA3R0
Index	2	1	0

STYLESHEETS CODE

Decorating your web pages

BELOW ARE SOME STYLESHEETS I COOKED UP THAT I LIKE AND THINK YOU MIGHT TOO. Don't worry I won't be offended if you take and modify to your hearts delight. Please do!

NONE

```
txtstream.WriteLine("<style type='text/css'>")
txtstream.WriteLine("th")
txtstream.WriteLine("{")
txtstream.WriteLine("    COLOR: darkred;")
txtstream.WriteLine("}")
txtstream.WriteLine("td")
txtstream.WriteLine("{")
txtstream.WriteLine("    COLOR: Navy;")
txtstream.WriteLine("}")
txtstream.WriteLine("</style>")
```

BLACK AND WHITE TEXT

```
txtstream.WriteLine("<style type='text/css'>")
txtstream.WriteLine("th")
txtstream.WriteLine("{")
txtstream.WriteLine("    COLOR: white;")
txtstream.WriteLine("    BACKGROUND-COLOR: black;")
```

```
txtstream.WriteLine("   FONT-FAMILY:font-family: Cambria, serif;")
txtstream.WriteLine("   FONT-SIZE: 12px;")
txtstream.WriteLine("   text-align: left;")
txtstream.WriteLine("   white-Space: nowrap;")
txtstream.WriteLine("}")
txtstream.WriteLine("td")
txtstream.WriteLine("{")
txtstream.WriteLine("   COLOR: white;")
txtstream.WriteLine("   BACKGROUND-COLOR: black;")
txtstream.WriteLine("   FONT-FAMILY: font-family: Cambria, serif;")
txtstream.WriteLine("   FONT-SIZE: 12px;")
txtstream.WriteLine("   text-align: left;")
txtstream.WriteLine("   white-Space: nowrap;")
txtstream.WriteLine("}")
txtstream.WriteLine("div")
txtstream.WriteLine("{")
txtstream.WriteLine("   COLOR: white;")
txtstream.WriteLine("   BACKGROUND-COLOR: black;")
txtstream.WriteLine("   FONT-FAMILY: font-family: Cambria, serif;")
txtstream.WriteLine("   FONT-SIZE: 10px;")
txtstream.WriteLine("   text-align: left;")
txtstream.WriteLine("   white-Space: nowrap;")
txtstream.WriteLine("}")
txtstream.WriteLine("span")
txtstream.WriteLine("{")
txtstream.WriteLine("   COLOR: white;")
txtstream.WriteLine("   BACKGROUND-COLOR: black;")
txtstream.WriteLine("   FONT-FAMILY: font-family: Cambria, serif;")
txtstream.WriteLine("   FONT-SIZE: 10px;")
txtstream.WriteLine("   text-align: left;")
txtstream.WriteLine("   white-Space: nowrap;")
txtstream.WriteLine("   display:inline-block;")
txtstream.WriteLine("   width: 100%;")
```

```
txtstream.WriteLine("}")
txtstream.WriteLine("textarea")
txtstream.WriteLine("{")
txtstream.WriteLine("   COLOR: white;")
txtstream.WriteLine("   BACKGROUND-COLOR: black;")
txtstream.WriteLine("   FONT-FAMILY: font-family: Cambria, serif;")
txtstream.WriteLine("   FONT-SIZE: 10px;")
txtstream.WriteLine("   text-align: left;")
txtstream.WriteLine("   white-Space: nowrap;")
txtstream.WriteLine("   width: 100%;")
txtstream.WriteLine("}")
txtstream.WriteLine("select")
txtstream.WriteLine("{")
txtstream.WriteLine("   COLOR: white;")
txtstream.WriteLine("   BACKGROUND-COLOR: black;")
txtstream.WriteLine("   FONT-FAMILY: font-family: Cambria, serif;")
txtstream.WriteLine("   FONT-SIZE: 10px;")
txtstream.WriteLine("   text-align: left;")
txtstream.WriteLine("   white-Space: nowrap;")
txtstream.WriteLine("   width: 100%;")
txtstream.WriteLine("}")
txtstream.WriteLine("input")
txtstream.WriteLine("{")
txtstream.WriteLine("   COLOR: white;")
txtstream.WriteLine("   BACKGROUND-COLOR: black;")
txtstream.WriteLine("   FONT-FAMILY: font-family: Cambria, serif;")
txtstream.WriteLine("   FONT-SIZE: 12px;")
txtstream.WriteLine("   text-align: left;")
txtstream.WriteLine("   display:table-cell;")
txtstream.WriteLine("   white-Space: nowrap;")
txtstream.WriteLine("}")
txtstream.WriteLine("h1 {")
txtstream.WriteLine("color: antiquewhite;")
```

```
txtstream.WriteLine("text-shadow: 1px 1px 1px black;")
txtstream.WriteLine("padding: 3px;")
txtstream.WriteLine("text-align: center;")
txtstream.WriteLine("box-shadow: inset 2px 2px 5px rgba(0,0,0,0.5), inset -
2px -2px 5px rgba(255,255,255,0.5)")
txtstream.WriteLine("}")
txtstream.WriteLine("</style>")
```

COLORED TEXT

```
txtstream.WriteLine("<style type='text/css'>")
txtstream.WriteLine("th")
txtstream.WriteLine("{")
txtstream.WriteLine("   COLOR: darkred;")
txtstream.WriteLine("   BACKGROUND-COLOR: #eeeeee;")
txtstream.WriteLine("   FONT-FAMILY:font-family: Cambria, serif;")
txtstream.WriteLine("   FONT-SIZE: 12px;")
txtstream.WriteLine("   text-align: left;")
txtstream.WriteLine("   white-Space: nowrap;")
txtstream.WriteLine("}")
txtstream.WriteLine("td")
txtstream.WriteLine("{")
txtstream.WriteLine("   COLOR: navy;")
txtstream.WriteLine("   BACKGROUND-COLOR: #eeeeee;")
txtstream.WriteLine("   FONT-FAMILY: font-family: Cambria, serif;")
txtstream.WriteLine("   FONT-SIZE: 12px;")
txtstream.WriteLine("   text-align: left;")
txtstream.WriteLine("   white-Space: nowrap;")
txtstream.WriteLine("}")
txtstream.WriteLine("div")
txtstream.WriteLine("{")
txtstream.WriteLine("   COLOR: white;")
txtstream.WriteLine("   BACKGROUND-COLOR: navy;")
```

```
txtstream.WriteLine("   FONT-FAMILY: font-family: Cambria, serif;")
txtstream.WriteLine("   FONT-SIZE: 10px;")
txtstream.WriteLine("   text-align: left;")
txtstream.WriteLine("   white-Space: nowrap;")
txtstream.WriteLine("}")
txtstream.WriteLine("span")
txtstream.WriteLine("{")
txtstream.WriteLine("   COLOR: white;")
txtstream.WriteLine("   BACKGROUND-COLOR: navy;")
txtstream.WriteLine("   FONT-FAMILY: font-family: Cambria, serif;")
txtstream.WriteLine("   FONT-SIZE: 10px;")
txtstream.WriteLine("   text-align: left;")
txtstream.WriteLine("   white-Space: nowrap;")
txtstream.WriteLine("   display:inline-block;")
txtstream.WriteLine("   width: 100%;")
txtstream.WriteLine("}")
txtstream.WriteLine("textarea")
txtstream.WriteLine("{")
txtstream.WriteLine("   COLOR: white;")
txtstream.WriteLine("   BACKGROUND-COLOR: navy;")
txtstream.WriteLine("   FONT-FAMILY: font-family: Cambria, serif;")
txtstream.WriteLine("   FONT-SIZE: 10px;")
txtstream.WriteLine("   text-align: left;")
txtstream.WriteLine("   white-Space: nowrap;")
txtstream.WriteLine("   width: 100%;")
txtstream.WriteLine("}")
txtstream.WriteLine("select")
txtstream.WriteLine("{")
txtstream.WriteLine("   COLOR: white;")
txtstream.WriteLine("   BACKGROUND-COLOR: navy;")
txtstream.WriteLine("   FONT-FAMILY: font-family: Cambria, serif;")
txtstream.WriteLine("   FONT-SIZE: 10px;")
txtstream.WriteLine("   text-align: left;")
```

```
txtstream.WriteLine("   white-Space: nowrap;")
txtstream.WriteLine("   width: 100%;")
txtstream.WriteLine("}")
txtstream.WriteLine("input")
txtstream.WriteLine("{")
txtstream.WriteLine("   COLOR: white;")
txtstream.WriteLine("   BACKGROUND-COLOR: navy;")
txtstream.WriteLine("   FONT-FAMILY: font-family: Cambria, serif;")
txtstream.WriteLine("   FONT-SIZE: 12px;")
txtstream.WriteLine("   text-align: left;")
txtstream.WriteLine("   display:table-cell;")
txtstream.WriteLine("   white-Space: nowrap;")
txtstream.WriteLine("}")
txtstream.WriteLine("h1 {")
txtstream.WriteLine("color: antiquewhite;")
txtstream.WriteLine("text-shadow: 1px 1px 1px black;")
txtstream.WriteLine("padding: 3px;")
txtstream.WriteLine("text-align: center;")
txtstream.WriteLine("box-shadow: inset 2px 2px 5px rgba(0,0,0,0.5), inset -
2px -2px 5px rgba(255,255,255,0.5)")
txtstream.WriteLine("}")
txtstream.WriteLine("</style>")
```

OSCILLATING ROW COLORS

```
txtstream.WriteLine("<style>")
txtstream.WriteLine("th")
txtstream.WriteLine("{")
txtstream.WriteLine("   COLOR: white;")
txtstream.WriteLine("   BACKGROUND-COLOR: navy;")
txtstream.WriteLine("   FONT-FAMILY:font-family: Cambria, serif;")
```

```
txtstream.WriteLine("   FONT-SIZE: 12px;")
txtstream.WriteLine("   text-align: left;")
txtstream.WriteLine("   white-Space: nowrap;")
txtstream.WriteLine("}")
txtstream.WriteLine("td")
txtstream.WriteLine("{")
txtstream.WriteLine("   COLOR: navy;")
txtstream.WriteLine("   FONT-FAMILY: font-family: Cambria, serif;")
txtstream.WriteLine("   FONT-SIZE: 12px;")
txtstream.WriteLine("   text-align: left;")
txtstream.WriteLine("   white-Space: nowrap;")
txtstream.WriteLine("}")
txtstream.WriteLine("div")
txtstream.WriteLine("{")
txtstream.WriteLine("   COLOR: navy;")
txtstream.WriteLine("   FONT-FAMILY: font-family: Cambria, serif;")
txtstream.WriteLine("   FONT-SIZE: 12px;")
txtstream.WriteLine("   text-align: left;")
txtstream.WriteLine("   white-Space: nowrap;")
txtstream.WriteLine("}")
txtstream.WriteLine("span")
txtstream.WriteLine("{")
txtstream.WriteLine("   COLOR: navy;")
txtstream.WriteLine("   FONT-FAMILY: font-family: Cambria, serif;")
txtstream.WriteLine("   FONT-SIZE: 12px;")
txtstream.WriteLine("   text-align: left;")
txtstream.WriteLine("   white-Space: nowrap;")
txtstream.WriteLine("   width: 100%;")
txtstream.WriteLine("}")
txtstream.WriteLine("textarea")
txtstream.WriteLine("{")
txtstream.WriteLine("   COLOR: navy;")
txtstream.WriteLine("   FONT-FAMILY: font-family: Cambria, serif;")
```

```
txtstream.WriteLine("    FONT-SIZE: 12px;")
txtstream.WriteLine("    text-align: left;")
txtstream.WriteLine("    white-Space: nowrap;")
txtstream.WriteLine("    display:inline-block;")
txtstream.WriteLine("    width: 100%;")
txtstream.WriteLine("}")
txtstream.WriteLine("select")
txtstream.WriteLine("{")
txtstream.WriteLine("    COLOR: navy;")
txtstream.WriteLine("    FONT-FAMILY: font-family: Cambria, serif;")
txtstream.WriteLine("    FONT-SIZE: 10px;")
txtstream.WriteLine("    text-align: left;")
txtstream.WriteLine("    white-Space: nowrap;")
txtstream.WriteLine("    display:inline-block;")
txtstream.WriteLine("    width: 100%;")
txtstream.WriteLine("}")
txtstream.WriteLine("input")
txtstream.WriteLine("{")
txtstream.WriteLine("    COLOR: navy;")
txtstream.WriteLine("    FONT-FAMILY: font-family: Cambria, serif;")
txtstream.WriteLine("    FONT-SIZE: 12px;")
txtstream.WriteLine("    text-align: left;")
txtstream.WriteLine("    display:table-cell;")
txtstream.WriteLine("    white-Space: nowrap;")
txtstream.WriteLine("}")
txtstream.WriteLine("h1 {")
txtstream.WriteLine("color: antiquewhite;")
txtstream.WriteLine("text-shadow: 1px 1px 1px black;")
txtstream.WriteLine("padding: 3px;")
txtstream.WriteLine("text-align: center;")
txtstream.WriteLine("box-shadow: inset 2px 2px 5px rgba(0,0,0,0.5), inset -2px -2px 5px rgba(255,255,255,0.5)")
txtstream.WriteLine("}")
```

```
txtstream.WriteLine("tr:nth-child(even){background-color:#f2f2f2;}")
txtstream.WriteLine("tr:nth-child(odd){background-color:#cccccc;
color:#f2f2f2;}")
txtstream.WriteLine("</style>")
```

GHOST DECORATED

```
txtstream.WriteLine("<style type='text/css'>")
txtstream.WriteLine("th")
txtstream.WriteLine("{")
txtstream.WriteLine("   COLOR: black;")
txtstream.WriteLine("   BACKGROUND-COLOR: white;")
txtstream.WriteLine("   FONT-FAMILY:font-family: Cambria, serif;")
txtstream.WriteLine("   FONT-SIZE: 12px;")
txtstream.WriteLine("   text-align: left;")
txtstream.WriteLine("   white-Space: nowrap;")
txtstream.WriteLine("}")
txtstream.WriteLine("td")
txtstream.WriteLine("{")
txtstream.WriteLine("   COLOR: black;")
txtstream.WriteLine("   BACKGROUND-COLOR: white;")
txtstream.WriteLine("   FONT-FAMILY: font-family: Cambria, serif;")
txtstream.WriteLine("   FONT-SIZE: 12px;")
txtstream.WriteLine("   text-align: left;")
txtstream.WriteLine("   white-Space: nowrap;")
txtstream.WriteLine("}")
txtstream.WriteLine("div")
txtstream.WriteLine("{")
txtstream.WriteLine("   COLOR: black;")
txtstream.WriteLine("   BACKGROUND-COLOR: white;")
txtstream.WriteLine("   FONT-FAMILY: font-family: Cambria, serif;")
txtstream.WriteLine("   FONT-SIZE: 10px;")
txtstream.WriteLine("   text-align: left;")
```

```
txtstream.WriteLine("  white-Space: nowrap;")
txtstream.WriteLine("}")
txtstream.WriteLine("span")
txtstream.WriteLine("{")
txtstream.WriteLine("  COLOR: black;")
txtstream.WriteLine("  BACKGROUND-COLOR: white;")
txtstream.WriteLine("  FONT-FAMILY: font-family: Cambria, serif;")
txtstream.WriteLine("  FONT-SIZE: 10px;")
txtstream.WriteLine("  text-align: left;")
txtstream.WriteLine("  white-Space: nowrap;")
txtstream.WriteLine("  display:inline-block;")
txtstream.WriteLine("  width: 100%;")
txtstream.WriteLine("}")
txtstream.WriteLine("textarea")
txtstream.WriteLine("{")
txtstream.WriteLine("  COLOR: black;")
txtstream.WriteLine("  BACKGROUND-COLOR: white;")
txtstream.WriteLine("  FONT-FAMILY: font-family: Cambria, serif;")
txtstream.WriteLine("  FONT-SIZE: 10px;")
txtstream.WriteLine("  text-align: left;")
txtstream.WriteLine("  white-Space: nowrap;")
txtstream.WriteLine("  width: 100%;")
txtstream.WriteLine("}")
txtstream.WriteLine("select")
txtstream.WriteLine("{")
txtstream.WriteLine("  COLOR: black;")
txtstream.WriteLine("  BACKGROUND-COLOR: white;")
txtstream.WriteLine("  FONT-FAMILY: font-family: Cambria, serif;")
txtstream.WriteLine("  FONT-SIZE: 10px;")
txtstream.WriteLine("  text-align: left;")
txtstream.WriteLine("  white-Space: nowrap;")
txtstream.WriteLine("  width: 100%;")
txtstream.WriteLine("}")
```

```
txtstream.WriteLine("input")
txtstream.WriteLine("{")
txtstream.WriteLine("   COLOR: black;")
txtstream.WriteLine("   BACKGROUND-COLOR: white;")
txtstream.WriteLine("   FONT-FAMILY: font-family: Cambria, serif;")
txtstream.WriteLine("   FONT-SIZE: 12px;")
txtstream.WriteLine("   text-align: left;")
txtstream.WriteLine("   display:table-cell;")
txtstream.WriteLine("   white-Space: nowrap;")
txtstream.WriteLine("}")
txtstream.WriteLine("h1 {")
txtstream.WriteLine("color: antiquewhite;")
txtstream.WriteLine("text-shadow: 1px 1px 1px black;")
txtstream.WriteLine("padding: 3px;")
txtstream.WriteLine("text-align: center;")
txtstream.WriteLine("box-shadow: inset 2px 2px 5px rgba(0,0,0,0.5), inset -2px -2px 5px rgba(255,255,255,0.5)")
txtstream.WriteLine("}")
txtstream.WriteLine("</style>")
```

3D

```
txtstream.WriteLine("<style type='text/css'>")
txtstream.WriteLine("body")
txtstream.WriteLine("{")
txtstream.WriteLine("   PADDING-RIGHT: 0px;")
txtstream.WriteLine("   PADDING-LEFT: 0px;")
txtstream.WriteLine("   PADDING-BOTTOM: 0px;")
txtstream.WriteLine("   MARGIN: 0px;")
txtstream.WriteLine("   COLOR: #333;")
txtstream.WriteLine("   PADDING-TOP: 0px;")
txtstream.WriteLine("   FONT-FAMILY: verdana, arial, helvetica, sans-serif;")
```

```
txtstream.WriteLine("}")
txtstream.WriteLine("table")
txtstream.WriteLine("{")
txtstream.WriteLine("   BORDER-RIGHT: #999999 3px solid;")
txtstream.WriteLine("   PADDING-RIGHT: 6px;")
txtstream.WriteLine("   PADDING-LEFT: 6px;")
txtstream.WriteLine("   FONT-WEIGHT: Bold;")
txtstream.WriteLine("   FONT-SIZE: 14px;")
txtstream.WriteLine("   PADDING-BOTTOM: 6px;")
txtstream.WriteLine("   COLOR: Peru;")
txtstream.WriteLine("   LINE-HEIGHT: 14px;")
txtstream.WriteLine("   PADDING-TOP: 6px;")
txtstream.WriteLine("   BORDER-BOTTOM: #999 1px solid;")
txtstream.WriteLine("   BACKGROUND-COLOR: #eeeeee;")
txtstream.WriteLine("   FONT-FAMILY: verdana, arial, helvetica, sans-serif;")
txtstream.WriteLine("   FONT-SIZE: 12px;")
txtstream.WriteLine("}")
txtstream.WriteLine("th")
txtstream.WriteLine("{")
txtstream.WriteLine("   BORDER-RIGHT: #999999 3px solid;")
txtstream.WriteLine("   PADDING-RIGHT: 6px;")
txtstream.WriteLine("   PADDING-LEFT: 6px;")
txtstream.WriteLine("   FONT-WEIGHT: Bold;")
txtstream.WriteLine("   FONT-SIZE: 14px;")
txtstream.WriteLine("   PADDING-BOTTOM: 6px;")
txtstream.WriteLine("   COLOR: darkred;")
txtstream.WriteLine("   LINE-HEIGHT: 14px;")
txtstream.WriteLine("   PADDING-TOP: 6px;")
txtstream.WriteLine("   BORDER-BOTTOM: #999 1px solid;")
txtstream.WriteLine("   BACKGROUND-COLOR: #eeeeee;")
txtstream.WriteLine("   FONT-FAMILY:font-family: Cambria, serif;")
txtstream.WriteLine("   FONT-SIZE: 12px;")
txtstream.WriteLine("   text-align: left;")
```

```
txtstream.WriteLine("    white-Space: nowrap;")
txtstream.WriteLine("}")
txtstream.WriteLine(".th")
txtstream.WriteLine("{")
txtstream.WriteLine("    BORDER-RIGHT: #999999 2px solid;")
txtstream.WriteLine("    PADDING-RIGHT: 6px;")
txtstream.WriteLine("    PADDING-LEFT: 6px;")
txtstream.WriteLine("    FONT-WEIGHT: Bold;")
txtstream.WriteLine("    PADDING-BOTTOM: 6px;")
txtstream.WriteLine("    COLOR: black;")
txtstream.WriteLine("    PADDING-TOP: 6px;")
txtstream.WriteLine("    BORDER-BOTTOM: #999 2px solid;")
txtstream.WriteLine("    BACKGROUND-COLOR: #eeeeee;")
txtstream.WriteLine("    FONT-FAMILY: font-family: Cambria, serif;")
txtstream.WriteLine("    FONT-SIZE: 10px;")
txtstream.WriteLine("    text-align: right;")
txtstream.WriteLine("    white-Space: nowrap;")
txtstream.WriteLine("}")
txtstream.WriteLine("td")
txtstream.WriteLine("{")
txtstream.WriteLine("    BORDER-RIGHT: #999999 3px solid;")
txtstream.WriteLine("    PADDING-RIGHT: 6px;")
txtstream.WriteLine("    PADDING-LEFT: 6px;")
txtstream.WriteLine("    FONT-WEIGHT: Normal;")
txtstream.WriteLine("    PADDING-BOTTOM: 6px;")
txtstream.WriteLine("    COLOR: navy;")
txtstream.WriteLine("    LINE-HEIGHT: 14px;")
txtstream.WriteLine("    PADDING-TOP: 6px;")
txtstream.WriteLine("    BORDER-BOTTOM: #999 1px solid;")
txtstream.WriteLine("    BACKGROUND-COLOR: #eeeeee;")
txtstream.WriteLine("    FONT-FAMILY: font-family: Cambria, serif;")
txtstream.WriteLine("    FONT-SIZE: 12px;")
txtstream.WriteLine("    text-align: left;")
```

txtstream.WriteLine("   white-Space: nowrap;")
txtstream.WriteLine("}")
txtstream.WriteLine("div")
txtstream.WriteLine("{")
txtstream.WriteLine("   BORDER-RIGHT: #999999 3px solid;")
txtstream.WriteLine("   PADDING-RIGHT: 6px;")
txtstream.WriteLine("   PADDING-LEFT: 6px;")
txtstream.WriteLine("   FONT-WEIGHT: Normal;")
txtstream.WriteLine("   PADDING-BOTTOM: 6px;")
txtstream.WriteLine("   COLOR: white;")
txtstream.WriteLine("   PADDING-TOP: 6px;")
txtstream.WriteLine("   BORDER-BOTTOM: #999 1px solid;")
txtstream.WriteLine("   BACKGROUND-COLOR: navy;")
txtstream.WriteLine("   FONT-FAMILY: font-family: Cambria, serif;")
txtstream.WriteLine("   FONT-SIZE: 10px;")
txtstream.WriteLine("   text-align: left;")
txtstream.WriteLine("   white-Space: nowrap;")
txtstream.WriteLine("}")
txtstream.WriteLine("span")
txtstream.WriteLine("{")
txtstream.WriteLine("   BORDER-RIGHT: #999999 3px solid;")
txtstream.WriteLine("   PADDING-RIGHT: 3px;")
txtstream.WriteLine("   PADDING-LEFT: 3px;")
txtstream.WriteLine("   FONT-WEIGHT: Normal;")
txtstream.WriteLine("   PADDING-BOTTOM: 3px;")
txtstream.WriteLine("   COLOR: white;")
txtstream.WriteLine("   PADDING-TOP: 3px;")
txtstream.WriteLine("   BORDER-BOTTOM: #999 1px solid;")
txtstream.WriteLine("   BACKGROUND-COLOR: navy;")
txtstream.WriteLine("   FONT-FAMILY: font-family: Cambria, serif;")
txtstream.WriteLine("   FONT-SIZE: 10px;")
txtstream.WriteLine("   text-align: left;")
txtstream.WriteLine("   white-Space: nowrap;")

txtstream.WriteLine("   display:inline-block;")
txtstream.WriteLine("   width: 100%;")
txtstream.WriteLine("}")
txtstream.WriteLine("textarea")
txtstream.WriteLine("{")
txtstream.WriteLine("   BORDER-RIGHT: #999999 3px solid;")
txtstream.WriteLine("   PADDING-RIGHT: 3px;")
txtstream.WriteLine("   PADDING-LEFT: 3px;")
txtstream.WriteLine("   FONT-WEIGHT: Normal;")
txtstream.WriteLine("   PADDING-BOTTOM: 3px;")
txtstream.WriteLine("   COLOR: white;")
txtstream.WriteLine("   PADDING-TOP: 3px;")
txtstream.WriteLine("   BORDER-BOTTOM: #999 1px solid;")
txtstream.WriteLine("   BACKGROUND-COLOR: navy;")
txtstream.WriteLine("   FONT-FAMILY: font-family: Cambria, serif;")
txtstream.WriteLine("   FONT-SIZE: 10px;")
txtstream.WriteLine("   text-align: left;")
txtstream.WriteLine("   white-Space: nowrap;")
txtstream.WriteLine("   width: 100%;")
txtstream.WriteLine("}")
txtstream.WriteLine("select")
txtstream.WriteLine("{")
txtstream.WriteLine("   BORDER-RIGHT: #999999 3px solid;")
txtstream.WriteLine("   PADDING-RIGHT: 6px;")
txtstream.WriteLine("   PADDING-LEFT: 6px;")
txtstream.WriteLine("   FONT-WEIGHT: Normal;")
txtstream.WriteLine("   PADDING-BOTTOM: 6px;")
txtstream.WriteLine("   COLOR: white;")
txtstream.WriteLine("   PADDING-TOP: 6px;")
txtstream.WriteLine("   BORDER-BOTTOM: #999 1px solid;")
txtstream.WriteLine("   BACKGROUND-COLOR: navy;")
txtstream.WriteLine("   FONT-FAMILY: font-family: Cambria, serif;")
txtstream.WriteLine("   FONT-SIZE: 10px;")

```
txtstream.WriteLine("    text-align: left;")
txtstream.WriteLine("    white-Space: nowrap;")
txtstream.WriteLine("    width: 100%;")
txtstream.WriteLine("}")
txtstream.WriteLine("input")
txtstream.WriteLine("{")
txtstream.WriteLine("    BORDER-RIGHT: #999999 3px solid;")
txtstream.WriteLine("    PADDING-RIGHT: 3px;")
txtstream.WriteLine("    PADDING-LEFT: 3px;")
txtstream.WriteLine("    FONT-WEIGHT: Bold;")
txtstream.WriteLine("    PADDING-BOTTOM: 3px;")
txtstream.WriteLine("    COLOR: white;")
txtstream.WriteLine("    PADDING-TOP: 3px;")
txtstream.WriteLine("    BORDER-BOTTOM: #999 1px solid;")
txtstream.WriteLine("    BACKGROUND-COLOR: navy;")
txtstream.WriteLine("    FONT-FAMILY: font-family: Cambria, serif;")
txtstream.WriteLine("    FONT-SIZE: 12px;")
txtstream.WriteLine("    text-align: left;")
txtstream.WriteLine("    display:table-cell;")
txtstream.WriteLine("    white-Space: nowrap;")
txtstream.WriteLine("    width: 100%;")
txtstream.WriteLine("}")
txtstream.WriteLine("h1 {")
txtstream.WriteLine("color: antiquewhite;")
txtstream.WriteLine("text-shadow: 1px 1px 1px black;")
txtstream.WriteLine("padding: 3px;")
txtstream.WriteLine("text-align: center;")
txtstream.WriteLine("box-shadow: inset 2px 2px 5px rgba(0,0,0,0.5), inset -2px -2px 5px rgba(255,255,255,0.5)")
txtstream.WriteLine("}")
txtstream.WriteLine("</style>")
```

SHADOW BOX

```
txtstream.WriteLine("<style type='text/css'>")
txtstream.WriteLine("body")
txtstream.WriteLine("{")
txtstream.WriteLine("   PADDING-RIGHT: 0px;")
txtstream.WriteLine("   PADDING-LEFT: 0px;")
txtstream.WriteLine("   PADDING-BOTTOM: 0px;")
txtstream.WriteLine("   MARGIN: 0px;")
txtstream.WriteLine("   COLOR: #333;")
txtstream.WriteLine("   PADDING-TOP: 0px;")
txtstream.WriteLine("   FONT-FAMILY: verdana, arial, helvetica, sans-serif;")
txtstream.WriteLine("}")
txtstream.WriteLine("table")
txtstream.WriteLine("{")
txtstream.WriteLine("   BORDER-RIGHT: #999999 1px solid;")
txtstream.WriteLine("   PADDING-RIGHT: 1px;")
txtstream.WriteLine("   PADDING-LEFT: 1px;")
txtstream.WriteLine("   PADDING-BOTTOM: 1px;")
txtstream.WriteLine("   LINE-HEIGHT: 8px;")
txtstream.WriteLine("   PADDING-TOP: 1px;")
txtstream.WriteLine("   BORDER-BOTTOM: #999 1px solid;")
txtstream.WriteLine("   BACKGROUND-COLOR: #eeeeee;")
txtstream.WriteLine("
filter:progid:DXImageTransform.Microsoft.Shadow(color='silver',     Direction=135,
Strength=16)")
txtstream.WriteLine("}")
txtstream.WriteLine("th")
txtstream.WriteLine("{")
txtstream.WriteLine("   BORDER-RIGHT: #999999 3px solid;")
txtstream.WriteLine("   PADDING-RIGHT: 6px;")
txtstream.WriteLine("   PADDING-LEFT: 6px;")
txtstream.WriteLine("   FONT-WEIGHT: Bold;")
```

```
txtstream.WriteLine("    FONT-SIZE: 14px;")
txtstream.WriteLine("    PADDING-BOTTOM: 6px;")
txtstream.WriteLine("    COLOR: darkred;")
txtstream.WriteLine("    LINE-HEIGHT: 14px;")
txtstream.WriteLine("    PADDING-TOP: 6px;")
txtstream.WriteLine("    BORDER-BOTTOM: #999 1px solid;")
txtstream.WriteLine("    BACKGROUND-COLOR: #eeeeee;")
txtstream.WriteLine("    FONT-FAMILY: font-family: Cambria, serif;")
txtstream.WriteLine("    FONT-SIZE: 12px;")
txtstream.WriteLine("    text-align: left;")
txtstream.WriteLine("    white-Space: nowrap;")
txtstream.WriteLine("}")
txtstream.WriteLine(".th")
txtstream.WriteLine("{")
txtstream.WriteLine("    BORDER-RIGHT: #999999 2px solid;")
txtstream.WriteLine("    PADDING-RIGHT: 6px;")
txtstream.WriteLine("    PADDING-LEFT: 6px;")
txtstream.WriteLine("    FONT-WEIGHT: Bold;")
txtstream.WriteLine("    PADDING-BOTTOM: 6px;")
txtstream.WriteLine("    COLOR: black;")
txtstream.WriteLine("    PADDING-TOP: 6px;")
txtstream.WriteLine("    BORDER-BOTTOM: #999 2px solid;")
txtstream.WriteLine("    BACKGROUND-COLOR: #eeeeee;")
txtstream.WriteLine("    FONT-FAMILY: font-family: Cambria, serif;")
txtstream.WriteLine("    FONT-SIZE: 10px;")
txtstream.WriteLine("    text-align: right;")
txtstream.WriteLine("    white-Space: nowrap;")
txtstream.WriteLine("}")
txtstream.WriteLine("td")
txtstream.WriteLine("{")
txtstream.WriteLine("    BORDER-RIGHT: #999999 3px solid;")
txtstream.WriteLine("    PADDING-RIGHT: 6px;")
txtstream.WriteLine("    PADDING-LEFT: 6px;")
```

```
txtstream.WriteLine("  FONT-WEIGHT: Normal;")
txtstream.WriteLine("  PADDING-BOTTOM: 6px;")
txtstream.WriteLine("  COLOR: navy;")
txtstream.WriteLine("  LINE-HEIGHT: 14px;")
txtstream.WriteLine("  PADDING-TOP: 6px;")
txtstream.WriteLine("  BORDER-BOTTOM: #999 1px solid;")
txtstream.WriteLine("  BACKGROUND-COLOR: #eeeeee;")
txtstream.WriteLine("  FONT-FAMILY: font-family: Cambria, serif;")
txtstream.WriteLine("  FONT-SIZE: 12px;")
txtstream.WriteLine("  text-align: left;")
txtstream.WriteLine("  white-Space: nowrap;")
txtstream.WriteLine("}")
txtstream.WriteLine("div")
txtstream.WriteLine("{")
txtstream.WriteLine("  BORDER-RIGHT: #999999 3px solid;")
txtstream.WriteLine("  PADDING-RIGHT: 6px;")
txtstream.WriteLine("  PADDING-LEFT: 6px;")
txtstream.WriteLine("  FONT-WEIGHT: Normal;")
txtstream.WriteLine("  PADDING-BOTTOM: 6px;")
txtstream.WriteLine("  COLOR: white;")
txtstream.WriteLine("  PADDING-TOP: 6px;")
txtstream.WriteLine("  BORDER-BOTTOM: #999 1px solid;")
txtstream.WriteLine("  BACKGROUND-COLOR: navy;")
txtstream.WriteLine("  FONT-FAMILY: font-family: Cambria, serif;")
txtstream.WriteLine("  FONT-SIZE: 10px;")
txtstream.WriteLine("  text-align: left;")
txtstream.WriteLine("  white-Space: nowrap;")
txtstream.WriteLine("}")
txtstream.WriteLine("span")
txtstream.WriteLine("{")
txtstream.WriteLine("  BORDER-RIGHT: #999999 3px solid;")
txtstream.WriteLine("  PADDING-RIGHT: 3px;")
txtstream.WriteLine("  PADDING-LEFT: 3px;")
```

```
txtstream.WriteLine("    FONT-WEIGHT: Normal;")
txtstream.WriteLine("    PADDING-BOTTOM: 3px;")
txtstream.WriteLine("    COLOR: white;")
txtstream.WriteLine("    PADDING-TOP: 3px;")
txtstream.WriteLine("    BORDER-BOTTOM: #999 1px solid;")
txtstream.WriteLine("    BACKGROUND-COLOR: navy;")
txtstream.WriteLine("    FONT-FAMILY: font-family: Cambria, serif;")
txtstream.WriteLine("    FONT-SIZE: 10px;")
txtstream.WriteLine("    text-align: left;")
txtstream.WriteLine("    white-Space: nowrap;")
txtstream.WriteLine("    display: inline-block;")
txtstream.WriteLine("    width: 100%;")
txtstream.WriteLine("}")
txtstream.WriteLine("textarea")
txtstream.WriteLine("{")
txtstream.WriteLine("    BORDER-RIGHT: #999999 3px solid;")
txtstream.WriteLine("    PADDING-RIGHT: 3px;")
txtstream.WriteLine("    PADDING-LEFT: 3px;")
txtstream.WriteLine("    FONT-WEIGHT: Normal;")
txtstream.WriteLine("    PADDING-BOTTOM: 3px;")
txtstream.WriteLine("    COLOR: white;")
txtstream.WriteLine("    PADDING-TOP: 3px;")
txtstream.WriteLine("    BORDER-BOTTOM: #999 1px solid;")
txtstream.WriteLine("    BACKGROUND-COLOR: navy;")
txtstream.WriteLine("    FONT-FAMILY: font-family: Cambria, serif;")
txtstream.WriteLine("    FONT-SIZE: 10px;")
txtstream.WriteLine("    text-align: left;")
txtstream.WriteLine("    white-Space: nowrap;")
txtstream.WriteLine("    width: 100%;")
txtstream.WriteLine("}")
txtstream.WriteLine("select")
txtstream.WriteLine("{")
txtstream.WriteLine("    BORDER-RIGHT: #999999 3px solid;")
```

```
txtstream.WriteLine("    PADDING-RIGHT: 6px;")
txtstream.WriteLine("    PADDING-LEFT: 6px;")
txtstream.WriteLine("    FONT-WEIGHT: Normal;")
txtstream.WriteLine("    PADDING-BOTTOM: 6px;")
txtstream.WriteLine("    COLOR: white;")
txtstream.WriteLine("    PADDING-TOP: 6px;")
txtstream.WriteLine("    BORDER-BOTTOM: #999 1px solid;")
txtstream.WriteLine("    BACKGROUND-COLOR: navy;")
txtstream.WriteLine("    FONT-FAMILY: font-family: Cambria, serif;")
txtstream.WriteLine("    FONT-SIZE: 10px;")
txtstream.WriteLine("    text-align: left;")
txtstream.WriteLine("    white-Space: nowrap;")
txtstream.WriteLine("    width: 100%;")
txtstream.WriteLine("}")
txtstream.WriteLine("input")
txtstream.WriteLine("{")
txtstream.WriteLine("    BORDER-RIGHT: #999999 3px solid;")
txtstream.WriteLine("    PADDING-RIGHT: 3px;")
txtstream.WriteLine("    PADDING-LEFT: 3px;")
txtstream.WriteLine("    FONT-WEIGHT: Bold;")
txtstream.WriteLine("    PADDING-BOTTOM: 3px;")
txtstream.WriteLine("    COLOR: white;")
txtstream.WriteLine("    PADDING-TOP: 3px;")
txtstream.WriteLine("    BORDER-BOTTOM: #999 1px solid;")
txtstream.WriteLine("    BACKGROUND-COLOR: navy;")
txtstream.WriteLine("    FONT-FAMILY: font-family: Cambria, serif;")
txtstream.WriteLine("    FONT-SIZE: 12px;")
txtstream.WriteLine("    text-align: left;")
txtstream.WriteLine("    display: table-cell;")
txtstream.WriteLine("    white-Space: nowrap;")
txtstream.WriteLine("    width: 100%;")
txtstream.WriteLine("}")
txtstream.WriteLine("h1 {")
```

```
txtstream.WriteLine("color: antiquewhite;")
txtstream.WriteLine("text-shadow: 1px 1px 1px black;")
txtstream.WriteLine("padding: 3px;")
txtstream.WriteLine("text-align: center;")
txtstream.WriteLine("box-shadow: inset 2px 2px 5px rgba(0,0,0,0.5), inset -2px -2px 5px rgba(255,255,255,0.5)")
txtstream.WriteLine("}")
txtstream.WriteLine("</style>")
```

www.ingramcontent.com/pod-product-compliance
Lightning Source LLC
LaVergne TN
LVHW041215050326
832903LV00021B/641